ESSENTIAL COMMODITIES ACT 1955- SUPREME COURT'S LATEST LEADING CASE LAWS

CASE NOTES- FACTS- FINDINGS OF APEX COURT JUDGES & CITATIONS

JAYPRAKASH BANSILAL SOMANI

Dedicated

To

All the Past & Present Judges of the Supreme Court of India.

Salute to their wisdom.

Salute to their interpretation of Law.

Salute to their elaborative judgement writing.

Supreme Court Of India.

Contents

Contents

Preface

Dear Learned Advocates ofTrial Court, High court and Supreme Court, Corporate and Individuals.

I am very delighted to provide you a book on ESSENTIAL COMMODITIES ACT 1955- SUPREME COURT'S LATEST LEADING CASE LAWS.

In this book you will get...

1. Name of the Case i. e. Cause title

2.Relevant Sections discussed in the case

3. Hon'ble Judges/Coram of the case

4.Number of PDF Pages in Original Judgement of the case

5. All available Citations of the case

6. Case Note with appeal allowed/ dismissed or disposed off

7. Facts of the case

8. Hon'ble Apex Court's findings, while dismissing/allowing or disposing the appeal

9. Ratio Decidendi if any.

My special thanks to Manupatra, because of their web portal I can compile this book in well manner. I am also thankful to Notion Press to support me to publish & market this book throughout the Country. Thanks to my Juniors, Advocate Colleagues & Insolvency Professional Colleagues to support me in this venture.

Adv. Manoj Kumar Chowdhary & Miss. Arvid Pooja Rai has helped me a lot to compile this book. I hope this book will add some value addition in the wealth of your legal knowledge. Your positive feedbacks will boost me to compile/ write further books & negative feedbacks will improve my skills. Kindly send your valuable feedbacks by email.

Thanks with Regards,

Jayprakash B. Somani

Advocate, Supreme Court of India

Email: jaysomani64@gmail.com

Web Site:www.jayprakashsomani.com

Call: 9322188701, 8459194576

Acknowledgements

Printed & Published by
Notion Press
No. 8, 3rd Cross Street,
CIT Colony, Mylapore,
Chennai, Tamil Nadu- 600004
Managed by
Jayprakash Somani Advocates & Solicitors
Law Firm for Supreme Court of India
Delhi Office
B- 851, 1st Floor, Shivaji Marg, New Ashok Nagar, Delhi 110096.
Call: 9322188701, 8459194576
Supreme Court Chamber
312, 3rd Floor, M. C. Setalvad Block, In front of 'D' Gate, Bhagwan Das
Road, Supreme Court of India, New Delhi 110001
Contact: 8459194576, 9811011747
www.jayprakashsomani.com
Download our app to get access to our Free Videos, Free Bare Acts,
Free Study Material in Legal as well as International Business Regime.
Android App Link ;-https://clpandrea.page.link/cmSm
Ios APp Link :-https://apps.apple.com/us/app/classplus/id1324522260
Login with org code ;- (qywzji)
Web Link ;-https://qywzji.courses.store/
Opportunity for Lawyers/ Social Workers to get Supreme Court Law
Firm JSAS's authorised centre at District Level.
Kindly Message or Call to: 9322188701
Books are available online in India
1.Notion Press:https://notionpress.com/author/jayprakash_somani
2.Amazon:https://www.amazon.in/s?k=jayprakash+somani
3.Flipkart:https://www.flipkart.com/search?q=Jayprakash%20Somani
Books are available online at International Market
4. Amazon International: https://www.amazon.com/
s?k=jayprakash+somani
5. Amazon United Kingdom: https://www.amazon.co.uk/
s?k=jayprakash+somani

ACKNOWLEDGEMENTS

6. E-Books/Kindle edition at National & International Level:
https://www.amazon.in/s?k=jaypraksh+somani

CHAPTER ONE

Sunil Kumar vs. State of Haryana (27.03.2012 - SC) : MANU/SC/0235/2012

Relative Section:

Code of Criminal Procedure, 1973 (CrPC) - Section 360; Code of Criminal Procedure, 1973 (CrPC) - Section 362; Constitution Of India - Article 142; Essential Commodities Act, 1955 - Section 7; Probation Of Offenders Act, 1958 - Section 4

Hon'bleJudges/Coram:

B.S. Chauhan and J.S. Khehar

Equivalent   Citation:

2012ACR1875,2012(113)AIC267,AIR2012SC1754,2013(1)AJR478, 2012(77)ACC 686 , 2012BomCR(Cri)82, II(2012)CCR104(SC), 2012(3)CLJ(SC)31, 2012CriLJ2093,

2012(2)Crimes69 (SC), 20 12 (2)J.L.J.R.278, 2012(2)JCC1392, [2012(2)JCR156(SC)], 2012(2)PLJR398, 2012(2)RCR (Criminal) 464, RL W2012(3)SC2535,RLW2012(4)SC305,RLW2012(4)SC3055,2012(4)SCALE21, (2012)5SCC398,(2012) 6SCC204

Case Reference:

P.N. Duda v. P. Shiv Shanker and Ors. MANU/SC/0362/1988 : AIR 1988 SC 1208;

Rathinam v. State of Tamil Nadu and Anr. MANU/SC/1978/2009 : (2011) 11 SCC 140;

State of Punjab v. Davinder Pal Singh Bhullar and Ors. etc. MANU/SC/ 1476/2011 : AIR 2012 SC 364;

Vishnu Agarwal v. State of U.P. and Anr. MANU/SC/0147/2011 : AIR 2011 SC 1232;

Kunhayammed and Ors. v. State of Kerala and Anr. MANU/SC/0432/2000 : (2000) 6 SCC 359;

Meghmala and Ors. v. G. Narasimha Reddy and Ors. MANU/SC/0608/2010 : (2010) 8 SCC 383;

Chhanni v. State of U.P. MANU/SC/8838/2006 : (2006) 5 SCC 396;

Dr. Buddhi Kota Subbarao v. K. Parasaran and Ors. MANU/SC/0678/1996 : AIR 1996 SC 2687;

Sabia Khan and Ors. v. State of U.P. and Ors. MANU/SC/0849/1999 : AIR 1999 SC 2284;

Abdul Rahman v. Prasony Bai and Anr. MANU/SC/1026/2002 : (2003) 1 SCC 488;

Issar Das v. The State of Punjab MANU/SC/0136/1972 : AIR 1972 SC 1295;

Precious Oil Corporation and Ors. v. State of Assam MANU/SC/0130/2009 : AIR 2009 SC 1566;

Pyarali K. Tejani v. Mahadeo Ramchandra Dange and Ors. MANU/SC/0146/1973 : AIR 1974 SC 228

NumberofPagesintheOriginalJudgment: 5

Case Note:

Food Adulteration- Benefit of Legislation - Section 360 of Code of Criminal Procedure, 1973 (CrPC); Section 4 of Probation of Offenders Act, 1958; Section 7 of Essential Commodities Act, 1955 - Petitioner's Application, for modifying order of trial Court, by giving him benefit of provisions of Section 360 of CrPC and/or Section 4 of 1958 Act, was dismissed by High Court - Hence, present Petition - Whether benefit of 1958 Act or Section 360 of CrPC, could be granted to Petitioner - Held, High Court rightly concluded that, Court could not entertain Petition having become functus officio - Petitioner being black-marketeer presumed that, he had a right to dictate terms to Court and get desired results, thus, approached this Court again and sought relief prayed before High Court - Petitioner had lost in four Courts earlier - Filing totally misconceived petition amounted to abuse of process of Court and waste of courts' time - Such litigant was not required to be dealt with lightly - Wherever Court came to conclusion that, process of Court was being abused, this Court would be justified in refusing to proceed further and refuse party from pursuing remedy in law - In case of M/s. Precious Oil Corp. and Ors. v.

State of Assam, this Court dealt with issue of application of 1958 Act in case of offences punishable under Section 7 of 1955 Act and held that, Kindly application of probation principle was negatived by imperatives of social defence and improbabilities of moral proselytisation - No chances could be taken by society with a man whose anti-social operations, disguised as a respectable trade, imperil numerous innocents - He was a security risk - These economic offences committed by white-collar criminals were unlikely to be dissuaded by gentle probationary process - Neither casual provocation nor motive against particular persons but planned profit-making from numbers of consumers furnished incentive - Thus, relief sought by Petitioner could not be granted - Petition was misconceived and untenable - Petition dismissed

Facts:

1. An FIR dated 15.9.1998 was lodged against the Petitioner and one other person under Section 7 of Essential Commodities Act, 1955 (hereinafter called the Act 1955) as they were found in possession of 1370 litres of blue kerosene and indulging in unauthorised sale thereof in violation of the provisions of Section 7 of the Act, 1955. After completing investigation charge sheet was filed and trial commenced.

2. The trial court vide judgment and order dated 27.10.1999/2.11.1999 found them guilty of the said offence and awarded sentence of imprisonment for one year alongwith a fine of Rs. 2,000/- each. Against the aforesaid order, the appeal of the Petitioner stood dismissed by the High Court vide judgment and order dated 30.7.2010. Petitioner preferred an application dated 25.7.2011 before the High Court for modifying the aforesaid judgment and order dated 30.7.2010 giving him the benefit of the provisions of Section 360 of Code of Criminal Procedure, 1973 (hereinafter called Code of Criminal Procedure.) and/or Section 4 of the Probation of Offenders Act, 1958 (hereinafter called the Act 1958). The said application was dismissed vide impugned order dated 19.9.2011.

3. It may be pertinent to mention that against the judgment and order dated 30.7.2010, the Petitioner had filed SLP (Crl.) No. 1469 of 2011 on 13.10.2011 which was dismissed by this Court vide order dated 27.1.2012. Subsequent thereto this special leave petition has been filed on 29.2.2012 challenging the order dated 19.9.2011. No explanation has been furnished as why the present petition could not be filed during the pendency of the earlier SLP or both the orders could not be challenged simultaneously as the order impugned herein had been passed much prior to the filing of the first

SLP on 13.10.2011, and Petitioner surrendered to serve out the sentence only on 13.1.2012.

4. The High Court dealt with various propositions of law while dealing with the averments raised on his behalf including the application of the provisions of Section 362 Code of Criminal Procedure. which puts a complete embargo on the criminal court to reconsider any case after delivery of the judgment as the court becomes functus officio.

Held by Hon'ble Court

1.Thus, in view of the above, the relief sought by the Petitioner cannot be granted. Petition is misconceived and untenable. The petition being devoid of any merit, is accordingly dismissed with the cost of Rs. 20,000/- which the Petitioner is directed to deposit within a period of four weeks with the Supreme Court Legal Services Authority and file proof thereof before the Registrar of this Court, failing which the matter be placed before the Court for appropriate direction for recovery.

CHAPTER TWO

West U.P. Sugar Mills Association and Ors. vs. The State of Uttar Pradesh and Ors. (22.04.2020 - SC) : MANU/SC/0381/2020

Relative Section:

Constitution of India - Article 14, Article 19(1), Article 31, Article 246, Article 254, Article 254(1), Article 254(2), Article 369; Criminal Law (Amendment) Act, 1952; Essential Commodities Act, 1955 - Section 2(a), Section 3(1), Section 3(3C), Section 16; Section 3; Section 4; Indian Penal Code, 1860 (IPC) - Section 161, 468, 471; Industries (Development and Regulation) Act, 1951 - Section 11(a), Section 12, Section 13; Prevention of Corruption Act, 1988 - Section 5(1), Section 5(2); Sugar and Gur Control Order, 1950; Sugar Industry (Protection) Act, 1932; Sugarcane Act, 1934 - Section 3(2); Tamil Nadu Public Men (Criminal Misconduct) Act, 1973; Uttar Pradesh Sugar Factories Control Act, 1938; Sugarcane (Control) Order, 1955; Sugarcane (Control) Order, 1966; Uttar Pradesh Sugarcane (Regulation of Supply and Purchase) Act, 1953 - Section 15, Section 16, Section 16(1), Section 16(2), Section 17, Section 26, Section 28; Uttar Pradesh Sugarcane (Regulation of Supply and Purchase) Order, 1954; Uttar Pradesh Sugarcane Rules, 1954 - Rule 20, Rule 94,Rule 106,Rule 107; Defence of India Act, 1915; Bihar Sugar Factories Control Act, 1937; Uttar Pradesh Sugar Factories Control (Amendment) Act, 1952; Uttar Pradesh

Ganna (Poorti Tatha Kharid Viniyaman) (Sanshodhan) Adhiniyam, 1963; Industries (Development and Regulation) Amendment Act, 1953; Constitution Third Amendment Act, 1954; India (Central Government and Legislature) Act, 1946.

Hon'bleJudges/Coram:

Arun Mishra, Indira Banerjee, Vineet Saran, M.R. Shah and Aniruddha Bose

Equivalent Citation: 2020(8)ADJ1, 2020 3 AWC2784SC, 2020(3)BLJ540, 2020/INSC/346, (2020)4MLJ384, (2020)9SCC548, [2020]9SCR530

Case Reference:

Ch. Tika Ramji and Ors. etc. v. The State of Uttar Pradesh and Ors. MANU/SC/0008/1956;

U.P. Co-operative Cane Unions Federations v. West U.P. Sugar Mills Association and Ors. etc. etc. MANU/SC/0455/2004;

State of Orissa v. M.A. Tulloch and Co. MANU/SC/0021/1963; M. Karunanidhi v. Union of India and Anr. MANU/SC/0159/1979;

Dr Preeti Srivastava and Anr. v. State of M.P. and Ors. MANU/SC/1021/1999;

Rajiv Sarin and Anr. v. State of Uttarakhand and Ors. MANU/SC/0913/2011;

The Belsund Sugar Co. Ltd. v. The State of Bihar & Ors. Etc. MANU/SC/0457/1999;

Punjab Dairy Development Board and Anr., etc. v. Cepham Milk Specialities Ltd. and Ors., etc. MANU/SC/0672/2004;

Southern Petrochemical Industries Co. Ltd. v. Electricity Inspector and E.T.I.O. and Ors. MANU/SC/2333/2007;

Bharat Hydro Power Corpn. Ltd. and Ors. v. State of Assam and Anr. MANU/SC/0010/2004;

Sukhnandan Saran Dinesh Kumar and Ors. v. Union of India (UOI) and Ors. MANU/SC/0020/1982;

G.P. Stewart v. B.K. Roy Chaudhury;

Shyamakant Lal v. Rambhajan Singh;

U.P. Cooperative Cane Unions Federations v. West U.P. Sugar Mills Association and Ors.

NumberofPagesintheOriginalJudgment: 38

Case Note:

Constitution - Fixation of price - Power thereto - Section 16 of U.P. Sugarcane Act, 1953 and Section 3(2)(c) of Essential Commodities Act, 1955 - This Court in Ch. Tika Ramji and Ors., Etc. v. The State of Uttar Pradesh and Ors. held that Section 16 of Act, 1953 does not include power to fix price and price of cane fixed by U.P. Government only mean price fixed by appropriate Government which would be Central Government - However, subsequently in case of U.P. Cooperative Cane Unions Federations v. West U.P. Sugar Mills Association and Ors., this Court held that State Government has power to fix price which may be higher than minimum price fixed by Central Government - Hence, present reference - Whether State of U.P. had authority to fix State Advised Price (SAP), which was required to be paid over and above minimum price fixed by Central Government.

Facts:

This Court in Ch. Tika Ramji and Ors., Etc. v. The State of Uttar Pradesh and Ors. held that Section 16 of the U.P. Sugarcane (Regulation of Supply and Purchase) Act, 1953 does not include the power to fix a price. The price of cane fixed by the U.P. Government only mean the price fixed by the appropriate Government which would be the Central Government, under Clause 3 of the Sugarcane (Control) Order, 1955. Even the provisions in behalf of the agreement contained in Clauses 3 and 4 of the U.P. Sugarcane (Regulation of Supply and Purchase) Order, 1954 provided that the price was to be the minimum price to be notified by the Government subject to such deduction, if any, as may be notified by the Government from time to time, meaning thereby the Central Government, the State Government not having made any provision in that behalf at any time whatsoever. However, subsequently, another five Judges Bench of this Court in the case of U.P. Coop. Cane Unions Federations had specifically gone into the question of repugnancy and held that the inconsistency or repugnancy will rise if the State Government fixes a price which is lower than that fixed by the Central Government. But, if the price fixed by the State Government is higher than that fixed by the Central Government, there will be no occasion for any inconsistency or repugnancy as it is possible for both the orders to operate simultaneously and to comply with both of them. A higher price fixed by the State Government would automatically comply with the provisions of Clause 3(2) of 1966 Order. Therefore, any price fixed by the State Government which is higher than that fixed by the Central Government cannot lead to any kind of repugnancy. In the case of U.P.

Coop. Cane Unions Federations, this Court held that the State Government has power to fix the price which may be higherthan the minimum price fixed by the Central Government.

Held, while answering the reference:

i. The relevant provisions which fell for consideration before this Court in the case of Tika Ramji and which fell for consideration by this Court in the case of U.P. Coop. Cane Unions Federations were altogether different. Clause 3 of 1955 Order empowered the Central Government to fix the price or the minimum price. The said Clause 3 of 1955 Order was under consideration by this Court in the case of Tika Ramji. However, subsequently, 1955 Order had been repealed by 1966 Order and Clause 3 of 1966 Order provides that the Central Government may fix the minimum price of the sugarcane. Therefore, when the legislature consciously deleted the word the price and retained the power with the Central Government to fix the minimum price, some meaning had to be given to such a deletion. The intention of the legislature was also required to be considered when certain words in the provisions of a statute are deleted or added and/or substituted. In the case of Tika Ramji, this Court though specifically observed and held that in the field of sugar and sugarcane, both, the Parliament and the State legislature would have the concurrent Jurisdiction as the same will fall under Entry 33 in the Concurrent List of seventh Schedule. Considering the fact that the State Government did not exercise the power of fixing the price, though the powers were available and the Central Government fixed the price/minimum price which came to be adopted by the State Government, this Court in Tika Ramji's case held that in such a situation there is no conflict and the question of repugnancy does not arise. Therefore, there was no apparent conflict between the decisions in Tika Ramji's case and U.P. Coop. Cane Unions Federations, which require to be referred to a larger Bench of seven Judges. [18]

ii. Considering the entire scheme of 1966 Order, it provides for the minimum price and the additional price or the advised price. Considering the said provisions under 1966 Order, there cannot be any sugarcane price (advised price) below the minimum price. As per the agreement entered into the advised price necessarily had to be higher than the minimum price. Thus, there was a difference between the price and the minimum price. As per Clause 3 of 1966 Order, it empowers the Central Government to fix the minimum price and the State Government was authorized to fix the Advised Price which was always higher than the minimum price fixed by the Central Government. Therefore, as rightly observed by this Court in the case of U.P. Coop. Cane Unions Federations, there was no conflict in exercise of powers by the Central Government in fixing the minimum price and in fixing the advised price by the State Government which was higher than the minimum price fixed by the Central Government. Therefore, as rightly observed by this Court in the case of U.P. Coop. Cane Unions Federations, there is no inconsistency or repugnancy in fixing the advised price or "remunerative price by the State Government and the minimum price fixed by the Central Government. As rightly held, if the price fixed by the State Government was higher than that fixed by the Central Government, there would be no occasion for any inconsistency or repugnancy as it is possible for both the orders to operate simultaneously and to comply with both of them. [22]

(iii) Thus, it was held that the view taken by the Constitution Bench of this Court in the subsequent decision in the case of U.P. Coop. Cane Unions Federations was the correct law. There was no conflict between the two decisions of this Court in the case of Tika Ramji and in the case of U.P. Coop. Cane Unions Federations and therefore, there is no necessity to refer the matter to the larger Bench consisting of seven Judges. Therefore, final conclusions were as under:

a. By virtue of Entries 33 and 34 List III of seventh Schedule, both the Central Government as well as the State Government had the power to fix the price of sugarcane. The Central Government having exercised the power and fixed the minimum price, the State Government could not fix the minimum price of sugarcane. However, at the same time, it was always open for the State Government to fix the advised price which was always higher than the minimum price, in view of the relevant provisions of the Sugarcane (Control) Order, 1966, which had been issued in exercise of powers under Section 16 of the U.P. Sugarcane (Regulation of Supply and Purchase) Act, 1953.

b. The Sugarcane (Control) Order, 1966 which had been issued Under Section 16 of the U.P. Sugarcane (Regulation of Supply and Purchase) Act, 1953 confers power upon the State Government to fix the remunerative/advised price at which sugarcane can be bought or sold which shall always be higher than the minimum price fixed by the Central Government.

c. Section 16 of the U.P. Sugarcane (Regulation of Supply and Purchase) Act, 1953 was not repugnant to Section 3(2)(c) of the Essential Commodities Act, 1955 and Clause 3 of the Sugarcane (Control) Order, 1966 as, the price which was fixed by the Central Government is the minimum price and the price which is fixed by the State Government was the advised price which was always higher than the minimum price fixed by the Central Government and therefore, there was no conflict. It was only in a case where the advised price fixed by the State Government was lower than the "minimum price" fixed by the Central Government, the provisions of the Central enactments will prevail and the minimum price fixed by the Central Government would prevail. So long as the advised price fixed by the State Government was higher than the minimum price fixed by the Central Government, the same could not be said to be void under Article 254 of the Constitution of India.

d. The view taken by the Constitution Bench of this Court in the case of U.P. Cooperative Cane Unions Federations v. West U.P. Sugar Mills Association and Ors. ws the correct law. [23]

Industry: Sugar

Shambhu Dayal Agarwala vs. State of West Bengal and Ors. (03.05.1990 - SC) : MANU/SC/0469/1990

Relative Section:

Essential Commodities Act, 1955 - Section 10A, Essential Commodities Act, 1955 - Section 11, Section 2, Section 2(f), Section 2(ia), Section 3, Section 6 Section 6-A,Section 6-C, Section 6A, Section 6B, Section 6C, Section 6D, Section 6E, Section 7, Section 8, Section 9, Section 7(1), Section 7(1)(b); Indian Penal Code 1860, (IPC) - Section 21; Section 452

Hon'bleJudges/Coram:

S. Ranganathan and A.M. Ahmadi, JJ.

Equivalent Citation: 1990(14) ACR438 (SC), 1990 (27) ACC 360, (1991)1CALLT1 (SC), 1990(2) Crimes665 (SC), JT1990(2) SC314, 1990(2)RCR (Criminal) 234, (1990)3SCC549, [1990] 2SCR987

Case Reference: nil

NumberofPagesintheOriginalJudgment:9

Case Note:

Criminal - seized goods - Sections 3, 6A, 6A (2), 6E, 7 and 7 (1) of Essential Commodities Act, 1955 - whether Collector entitled to release seized goods to owner during pendency of proceedings before Court - under Section 6-A and 6-E Collector had no power to Order release of seized commodity - word release is used in Act in limited sense of release for sale and not return to owner.

Facts:

The petitioner being engaged in the manufacture of mustard oil at his factory at 1, Canal Road, Police Station Behala, Calcutta-53, was required to maintain a stock of mustard seed at his factory premises. A contingent of officers of the District Enforcement Branch led by the Investigating Officer Gopal Mosat, the complainant, raided the factory premises of the petitioner on the morning of Sunday, September 20, 1987, in the absence of the petitioner. The said raid continued till the early hours of September 21, 1987. During the said raid 562 bags of Mustard Seeds and 267 tins of Mustard Oil, weighing about 39.92 quintals, were seized lor purported infraction of the conditions of the licence as well as the orders issued under Section 3 of the Act. The Investigating Officer filed a written complaint in that behalf at the Behala Police Station which came to be treated as the First Information Report. The report of the seizure of the essential commodity was made to the concerned Collector as required by Section 6A of the Act for initiating confiscation proceedings. On September 27, 1987, a charge-sheet was filed before the learned Special Judge. It may be mentioned that before the submission of the charge-sheet a Writ Petition was filed in the High Court wherein certain interim orders were made with which we are not concerned. Suffice it to say that the said Writ Petition was disposed of by a learned Single Judge of the High Court on February 2, 1988, reserving liberty to the petitioner to apply for release of the seized goods to the Collector before whom the confiscation proceedings were pending. Thereupon, the petitioner preferred an application on February 9, 1988 under Section 6E of the Act before the Additional Collector for release of the seized commodities. On March 11, 1988 the said officer dropped the confiscation proceedings, albeit without prejudice to the prosecution pending before the Special Judge, and directed the release of the seized commodities. Feeling aggrieved by the said order of release, the State Government invoked the revisional jurisdiction of the High Court. The said Criminal Revision No. 402 of 1988 was allowed by the High Court on May 11, 1988. The High Court set aside the impugned order of release of the seized goods holding that under the provisions of Section 6A read with Section 6E of the Act, the Collector had no power to order release of the seized commodity. The High Court approached the question thus:

Held by Hon'ble Court

Counsel for the appellant next pointed out that this Court had passed an interim order on December 8, 1988 for sale of the seized commodity and for handing over the sale proceeds to the appellant on the latter furnishing a bank guarantee to the satisfaction of the Special Judge, 24 Paraganas (South), Alipore. Despite this order the seized commodity had not been disposed of Mr. Rao, therefore, contended that this Court should not assist the respondent State which had denied and thwarted the order of this Court. It is true that the seized commodity has not been disposed of to-date. But it appears from the subsequent order of February 13, 1989 as amended by the order of February 15, 1989, that the only direction given to the Special Judge was to dispose of the pending prosecution within two months. It was further directed that the Special Judge will pass appropriate consequential orders regarding the release of the seized goods. It, therefore, becomes clear that when the subsequent orders were passed on February 13 and 15, 1989, the appellant did not insist on the sale of the seized commodity as per the order of December 8, 1988. The matter came up for hearing on subsequent occasions also but at no time did the appellant press for the implementation of the said order of December 8, 1988. Even after the Special Judge recorded an acquittal and directed return of the goods, the appellant did not seek implementation of the said order. Nor did the appellant move the High Court for the implementation of the said order in the appeal pending against the order of acquittal . It is, therefore, too late in the day now to contend that as the order of December 8, 1988 has remained unimplemented we should refuse to grant any relief to the respondent State.

For the reasons stated above we see no merit in this appeal and dismiss the same with costs.

CHAPTER FOUR

63 Moons Technologies Ltd. and Ors. vs. Union of India (UOI) and Ors. (30.04.2019 - SC) : MANU/SC/0629/2019

Relative Section:

Companies Act, 1956 - Section 209A, Section 211,Section 217, Section 292A,Section 235, Section 236,Section 237,Section 391,Section 392,Section 393,Section 394,Section 395, Section 396, Section 396(1), Section 396(3), Section 396(3A), Section 396(4), Section 396(5); Maharashtra Protection of Interest of Depositors Act, 1999 - Section 4, Section 5; Securities and Exchange Board of India Act, 1992 - Section 27; Banking Regulation Act, 1949 - Section 45, Banking Regulation Act, 1949 - Section 45(1), Section 45(2), Section 45(4),Section 45(11); Jammu and Kashmir Agrarian Reforms Act, 1976; Uttar Pradesh Zamindari Abolition and Land Reforms Act, 1950 - Section 90; Essential Commodities Act, 1955 - Section 3; Constitution (First Amendment) Act, 1951; Banking Companies (Acquisition and Transfer of Undertakings) Act, 1980 - Section 9; Companies (Amendment) Act, 1960; Indian Electricity Act, 1910 - Section 3(2); Gujarat Town Planning and Urban Development Act, 1976 - Section 17,Section 17(1); Customs Act, 1962 - Section 25(2); Prevention of Corruption Act, 1988 - Section 3(1); Motor Vehicles Act, 1939 - Section 43A, Section 43A(1); Forward Contracts (Regulation) Act, 1952; Indian Penal Code, 1860 (IPC); Code of Civil Procedure, 1908 (CPC) - Order 1 Rule 8; Constitution of India - Article 12, Article 13, Article 13(3), Article 14, Constitution of India - Article 19, Article 19(1), Article 21, Article 31,

Article 31A, Article 31B, Article 226, Article 300A; Indian Electricity (Uttar Pradesh Sanshodhan) Adhiniyam, 1961.

Hon'bleJudges/Coram:

Rohinton Fali Nariman and Vineet Saran

Equivalent Citation: Equivalent Citation: [2019]150CLA209(SC), [2019]217CompCas181(SC), (2020)1CompLJ229(SC), 2019/INSC/597, 2019(7)SCALE50, (2019)18SCC401, [2019]8SCR26

NumberofPagesintheOriginalJudgment: 66

Case Reference:

Ganesh Bank of Kurundwad Ltd. v. Union of India MANU/SC/3707/2006 : (2006) 10 SCC 645;

Mohinder Singh Gill v. Chief Election Commissioner MANU/SC/0209/1977 : (1978) 1 SCC 405;

K.I. Shephard v. Union of India MANU/SC/0643/1987 : (1987) 4 SCC 431 : 1987 SCC (L&S) 438 : (1988) 1 SCR 188;

J.K. (Bombay) (P) Ltd. v. New Kaiser-i-Hind Spinning and Weaving Co. Ltd. MANU/SC/0217/1968 : (1969) 2 SCR 866;

Bacha F. Guzdar v. Commissioner of Income Tax MANU/SC/0072/1954 : (1955) 1 SCR 876;

Union of India v. G. Ganayutham MANU/SC/0834/1997 : (1997) 7 SCC 463;

Om Kumar v. Union of India MANU/SC/0704/2000 : (2001) 2 SCC 386;

Barium Chemicals Ltd. and Anr. v. Company Law Board MANU/SC/0037/1966 : (1966) Supp SCR 311;

Rohtas Industries Ltd. v. S.D. Agarwal MANU/SC/0020/1968 : (1969) 3 SCR 108;

Haryana Financial Corporation v. Jagdamba Oil Mills MANU/SC/0056/2002 : (2002) 3 SCC 496;

Prem Nath Raina v. State of Jammu & Kashmir and Ors. MANU/SC/0069/1983 : (1983) 4 SCC 616;

Waman Rao v. Union of India MANU/SC/0091/1980 : (1981) 2 SCC 362 : AIR 1981 SC 271: (1981) 2 SCR 1;

Budhan Singh and Anr. v. Nabi Bux and Anr. MANU/SC/0353/1969 : (1970) 2 SCR 10;

Prag Ice & Oil Mills v. Union of India MANU/SC/0493/1978 : (1978) 3 SCC 459;

Union of India and Anr. v. Cynamide India Ltd. and Anr. MANU/SC/0076/1987 : (1987) 2 SCC 720;

New Bank of India Employees' Union and Anr. v. Union of India and Ors. MANU/SC/0858/1996 : (1996) 8 SCC 407;

Quarry Owners' Association v. State of Bihar and Ors. MANU/SC/0504/2000 : (2000) 8 SCC 655;

Thomas Dana v. State of Punjab MANU/SC/0140/1958 : (1959) Supp (1) SCR 274;

Hamdard Dawakhana (Wakf) Lal Kuan, Delhi and Anr. v. Union of India and Ors. MANU/SC/0016/1959 : (1960) 2 SCR 671;

Ram Singh v. State of Delhi MANU/SC/0005/1951 : (1951) SCR 451;

Express Newspapers (Private) Ltd. v. Union of India MANU/SC/0157/1958 : (1959) SCR 12;

Sakal Papers (P) Ltd. and Ors. v. Union of India MANU/SC/0090/1961 : (1962) 3 SCR 842;

Dwarkadas Shrinivas v. Sholapur Spinning & Weaving Co. Ltd. MANU/SC/0019/1953 : (1954) SCR 674;

Ajay Hasia and Ors. v. Khalid Mujib Sehravardi and Ors. MANU/SC/0498/1980 : (1981) 1 SCC 722;

M.C. Mehta and Anr. v. Union of India and Ors. (Shriram-Oleum Gas) MANU/SC/0092/1986 : (1987) 1 SCC 395;

Western U.P. Electric Power & Supply Co. Ltd. v. State of U.P. and Anr. (1969) 1 SCC 817;

Rampur Distillery Co. Ltd. v. Company Law Board MANU/SC/0612/1969 : (1970) 2 SCR 177;

M.A. Rasheed and Ors. v. State of Kerala MANU/SC/0051/1974 : (1975) 2 SCR 93;

Khudiram Das v. State of West Bengal MANU/SC/0423/1974 : (1975) 2 SCC 81;

Emperor v. Shibnath Bannerji MANU/FE/0010/1943 : AIR 1943 FC 75 : 1944 FCR 1 : 45 Cri. LJ 341;

Commissioner of Police v. Gordhandas Bhanji MANU/SC/0002/1951 : AIR 1952 SC 16 : 1952 SCR 135;

Simms Motor Units Ltd. v. Minister of Labour and National Service (1946) 2 All ER 201;

Machindar v. King MANU/FE/0008/1950 : AIR 1950 FC 129 : 51 Cri. LJ 1480 : 1949 FCR 827;

Pratap Singh v. State of Punjab MANU/SC/0272/1963 : AIR 1964 SC 72 : (1964) 4 SCR 733;

Tata Cellular v. Union of India MANU/SC/0002/1996 : (1994) 6 SCC 651;

R. v. Secretary of State for the Home Department, ex Brind MANU/UKHL/0008/1991 : (1991) 1 AC 696;

Bhikhubhai Vithlabhai Patel v. State of Gujarat MANU/SC/7399/2008 : (2008) 4 SCC 144;

M. Jhangir Bhatusha and Ors. v. Union of India and Ors. MANU/SC/0291/1989 : 1989 Supp (2) SCC 201;

J. Jayalalitha v. Union of India MANU/SC/0338/1999 : (1999) 5 SCC 138;

State of Bihar v. Maharajadhiraja Sir Kameshwar Singh of Darbhanga and Ors. MANU/SC/0019/1952 : (1952) 3 SCR 889;

Manimegalai v. Special Tehsildar (Land Acquisition Officer) Adi Dravidar Welfare MANU/SC/0382/2018 : (2018) 13 SCC 491;

Rameshwar Prasad and Ors. v. State of U.P. and Ors. MANU/SC/0266/1983 : (1983) 2 SCC 195;

Janata Dal v. H.S. Chowdhary and Ors. MANU/SC/0532/1992 : (1992) 4 SCC 305; R. v. Bedfordshire 24 LJ QB 84;

Municipal Corporation of the City of Ahmedabad and Ors. v. Jan Mohd. Usmanbhai and Anr. MANU/SC/0099/1986 : (1986) 3 SCC 20;

B.P. Sharma v. Union of India and Ors. MANU/SC/0598/2003 : (2003) 7 SCC 309; State of Maharashtra v. Himmatbhai Narbheram Rao MANU/SC/0321/1968 : AIR 1970 SC 1157 : (1969) 2 SCR 392;

State of Assam v. Sristikar Dowerah AIR 1957 SC 414;

Union of India v. Bhanamal Gulzarimal Ltd. MANU/SC/0046/1959 : AIR 1960 SC 475 : 1960 Cri. LJ 664;

Hindustan Lever Employees' Union v. Hindustan Lever Ltd. and Ors. MANU/SC/0101/1995 : 1995 Supp (1) SCC 499;

In Re: Hoare & Co. Ltd. 1933 All ER Rep 105;

In Re: Bugle Press Ltd. 1961 Ch 270 : (1960) 1 All ER 768 : (1960) 2 WLR 658; Bihar Public Service Commission v. Saiyed Hussain Abbas Rizwi and Anr. MANU/SC/1103/2012 : (2012) 13 SCC 61;

State of Bihar v. Kameshwar Singh MANU/SC/0020/1952 : AIR 1952 SC 252;

R.R. Tripathi v. Union of India MANU/MH/0614/2009 : (2010) 1 Bom CR 513;

Chairman, All India Railway Recruitment Board and Anr. v. K. Shyam Kumar and Ors. MANU/SC/0342/2010 : (2010) 6 SCC 614;

Madhyamic Shiksha Mandal, M.P. v. Abhilash Shiksha Prasar Samiti
MANU/SC/1453/1998 : (1998) 9 SCC 236;

PRP Exports and Ors. v. Chief Secretary, Government of Tamil Nadu and
Ors. MANU/SC/1290/2013 : (2014) 13 SCC 692;

Life Insurance Corporation of India v. Escorts Ltd. and Ors. MANU/SC/
0015/1985 : (1986) 1 SCC 264;

Commissioner of Income Tax (Central) Calcutta v. Standard Vacuum Oil
Co. MANU/SC/0127/1965 : (1966) 2 SCR 367;

Miheer H. Mafatlal v. Mafatlal Industries Ltd. MANU/SC/2143/1996 :
(1997) 1 SCC 579;

Institute of Chartered Accountants of India v. L.K. Ratna and Ors.
MANU/SC/0083/1986 : (1986) 3 SCR 1049;

Leary v. National Union of Vehicle Builders (1971) 1 Ch. 34;

In Re: Cardinal and Board of Commissioners of Police of City of
Cornwall (1974) 42 D.L.R. (3d) 323;

Wislang v. Medical Practitioners Disciplinary Committee (1974) 1
N.Z.L.R. 29;

Reid v. Rowley (1977) 2 N.Z.L.R. 472;

Union Carbide Corporation v. Union of India MANU/SC/0058/1992 :
(1991) Supp (1) SCR 251;

Charan Lal Sahu v. Union of India MANU/SC/0285/1990 : (1990) 1 SCC
613

Case Note:

Company - Amalgamation order - Challenge thereto -Articles 19, 14 and
Article 31A of Constitution of India, 1950 and Section 396 of Companies
Act, 1956 - Present batch of appeals and writ petition raised questions as to
applicability and construction of Section 396 of Act, 1956, which dealt with
compulsory amalgamation of companies by a Central Government order,
when this became essential in public interest - Whether final amalgamation
order was ultra vires Section 396 of the Companies Act, and violative of
Article 14 of Constitution of India.

Facts:

The Appellant, 63 Moons Technologies Ltd. (FTIL, which name was
changed to 63 Moons Technologies Ltd.), is a 99.99% shareholder of the
National Spot Exchange Ltd. (NSEL), and is a listed company. About 45%
of the shareholding of FTIL is held by Shri Jignesh Shah and family, and
about 43% of the shareholding is held by members of the Indian public.
Approximately 5% of the shareholding is held by institutional investors.

FTIL is a profitable company, having a positive net worth of over INR 2500 crore, and is in the business of providing software which is used for trading by brokers and exchanges across the country. FTIL has about 900 employees, and a Board of Directors which is different from the Board of Directors of its wholly owned subsidiary, i.e., NSEL. On the other hand, NSEL was incorporated in 2005 by Multi Commodities Exchanges [MCX] and its nominees. Ministry of Finance, Government of India, issued a notification withdrawing the exemption granted to NSEL. Exemptions granted to the National Commodity and Derivatives Exchange Ltd. (NCDEX) Spot Exchange and the National Agricultural Produce Market Committee (APMC) were also withdrawn. Additional Secretary, Department of Economic Affairs, wrote a letter to the Ministry of Corporate Affairs stating that FTIL and NSEL appear to be maintaining separate identities for a fraudulent purpose, i.e., to deprive investors of their money. As a result, there is a need to lift the corporate veil in order to unearth the fraud, as a result of which, amalgamation of two companies, where one has defrauded market participants and the other company is cash-rich and capable of addressing the payment crisis more effectively. It was therefore proposed to merge FTIL and NSEL under Section 396 of the Companies Act. On 21st October, 2014, a draft order of amalgamation, made in accordance with Section 396(3) of the Companies Act, was circulated to the relevant stakeholders. As a result, FTIL filed Writ Petition. Bombay High Court directed the parties to maintain status quo. Union of India filed an affidavit in reply, categorically confirming that the impugned draft order has been made by the Central Government on the basis of the FMC's proposal dated 18.08.2014. Bombay High Court vacated the status quo order, and passed an order allowing FTIL, NSEL, and their shareholders to file their objections to the draft amalgamation order. Meanwhile, Under Section 396(3), a compensation order was made, which involved compensation only to a particular shareholder of NSEL. Central Government issued a notification to merge the functions of the FMC with the Securities and Exchange Board of India [SEBI]. On the same day, the FCRA was also repealed. Thus, SEBI was now vested with the powers of the FMC which is to be governed by the Securities and Exchange Board of India Act, 1992 [SEBI Act]. Final amalgamation order was passed in terms of Section 396(3), thereby merging FTIL and NSEL, wherein all assets and liabilities of NSEL would become assets and liabilities of FTIL.

Held, while allowing the appeal

1. Section 396 cannot be challenged on the ground of Article 14 or Article 19, given Article 31A of the Constitution of India. However, this does not mean that, Section 396 must be construed in such a fashion that, it would lead to arbitrary or unreasonable results. [23]

2. In the context of compulsory amalgamation of two or more companies, the expression "public interest" would mean the welfare of the public or the interest of society as a whole, as contrasted with the "selfish" interest of a group of private individuals. "Public interest" would mean the combining of resources of two or more companies so as to impact production and consumption of goods and services and employment of persons relatable thereto for the general benefit of the community. Conversely, any action that impedes promotion of industry or obstructs growth which is in national or public interest would run counter to public interest. [54]

3. Neither FTIL nor NSEL has denied the fact that paired contracts in commodities were going on, and by April to July, 2013, 99% (and excluding E-series contracts), at least 46% of the turnover of NSEL was made up of such paired contracts. There is no doubt that, such paired contracts were, in fact, financing transactions which were distinct from sale and purchase transactions in commodities and were, thus, in breach of both the exemptions granted to NSEL, and the FCRA. NSEL throughout kept representing that it was, in fact, a commodity exchange dealing with spot deliveries. Apart from the Grant Thornton report and the FMC order, Shri Jignesh Shah, on 10.07.2013, made representations to the DCA and the FMC, in which he stated that, NSEL had full stock as collateral; 10-20% of open position as margin money; and that the stock currently held in NSEL's 120 warehouses was valued at INR 6000 crore, all of which turned out to be incorrect. Further, there is no doubt whatsoever that in July, 2013, as a result of NSEL stopping trading on its exchange, a payment crisis of approximately INR 5600 crore arose. [55.3]

4. When it comes to whether the Central Government's satisfaction as to whether it was "essential" to amalgamate companies, it must be borne in mind is that, NSEL had itself offered a settlement scheme to pay back the persons who have allegedly been duped. It was found that this scheme could not really take off, as a result of which, large amounts continued to be owed to such persons. That this was the real concern of the FMC is clear from a letter dated 18th August, 2014 addressed by thc FMC to the Secretary, Ministry of Corporate Affairs. This letter would show that the immediate

reason for amalgamation, according to the FMC, and which was faithfully carried out by Government, is that NSEL, as a corporate entity, seems financially and physically incapable of effecting any substantial recovery from defaulting members. This was the "emergency situation" according to the FMC, which should lead to an order of amalgamation of the holding and subsidiary companies so that the holding company's financial resources could be used to pursue proceedings by which monies owed to the alleged duped investors/traders could be recovered. [56]

5. What concerned the FMC in August 2014 has, by the date of the final amalgamation order, been largely redressed without amalgamation. The "emergency situation" of 2013 which, even according to the Central Government, required the emergent step of compulsory amalgamation has, by the time of the passing of the Central Government order, disappeared. What was emergent, and therefore, essential, even according to the FMC and the Government in 2013-2014, has been largely redressed in 2016, by the time the amalgamation order was made. Also, the Central Government order does not apply its mind to the essentiality aspect of Section 396 at all. In fact, in several places, it refers to "essential public interest" as if "essential" goes with "public interest" instead of being a separate and distinct condition precedent to the exercise of power Under Section 396. On facts, therefore, it is clear that the essentiality test, which is the condition precedent to the applicable to Section 396, cannot be said to have been satisfied. [56.2]

6. All the expressions used in relation to "public interest" have relation only to the businesses of the two companies that are sought to be amalgamated. There is no interest of the general public as opposed to the businesses of the two companies that are referred to. Leveraging of combined assets, capital, and reserves is only to settle liabilities of certain stakeholders and creditors when the order is read as a whole, and given the fact that the businesses of the two companies were completely different. So far as achieving economy of scale and efficient administration is concerned, it is difficult to see how this would apply to the fact situation in present case where NSEL is admittedly a company which has stopped functioning as a commodities exchange at least with effect from July, 2013 with no hope of any revival. Thus, the consolidation of businesses spoken about does not exist as a matter of fact, as NSEL's business has come to a grinding halt, as has been observed by the FMC and the Central Government itself. [59]

7. Recommendations are in the form of a letter dated 18.08.2014, in which the "business reality" is the fact that dues of INR 5600 crore have to be paid, and that NSEL does not have the wherewithal to do so. Thus, its parent company's financial resources ought to be used to effect such payment. This "business reality", therefore, speaks only of the private interest of the investors/traders who have been allegedly duped (which fact will only be established in suits filed by them in 2014), and nothing beyond (which would show some vestige of public interest). There is no "adjudication" on the "fraud" in the facts of the present case, and thus, not an exercise of lifting of the corporate veil of the pre-amalgamation companies. The amalgamation order contradicts itself by then stating that NSEL is the alter ego of FTIL, and thus, the two companies are practically one entity. In any event, these paragraphs do not indicate as to how the 'alter ego' argument impacts public interest. [59.3]

8. Under Section 396(4)(b), the Central Government may, after considering suggestions and objections from the stakeholders mentioned, make modifications in the draft order as may seem to it desirable. No modification has been made in the body of the Central Government order as finally made. If the Central Government had actually considered that each of these three reasons impact public interest, it would have explicitly said so after suggestions and objections were made by the various stakeholders. The fact that the Central Government has not amended the body of the final order is of great significance - it is only the original reasons given in the draft order that continue as such in the final order which, are not in furtherance of public interest at all. [59.4]

9. "Restoring/safeguarding public confidence in forward contracts and exchanges, which are an integral and essential part of the Indian economy and financial system, by consolidating the businesses of NSEL and FTIL," is not contained in the answer given to objections in the order. First and foremost, restoring public confidence is no part of the order. Similarly, when it comes to reason (b), "giving effect to business realities of the case" contained in the answer to objections does not contain "by consolidating the businesses of FTIL and NSEL", nor does it contain "and preventing FTIL from distancing itself from NSEL, which is, even otherwise, its alter ego". On the contrary, the High Court itself mentions, that "this is also not a case where the Central Government has, in fact, lifted the corporate veil, despite the alleged non-existence of the circumstances justifying lifting of such corporate veil", and further, "this is not a case where the Central

Government has lifted the corporate veil and sought to apportion any liability upon either NSEL or FTIL". No reasonable body of persons properly instructed in law could possibly arrive at the conclusion that the impugned order has been made in public interest. [59.5]

10. It is the Central Government that has to be "satisfied" that its order is in public interest and such "satisfaction" must, therefore, be of the Central Government itself and must, therefore, appear from the order itself. [63]

11. Section 396(3) speaks of a shareholder's or a creditor's interest in or rights against the company resulting from an amalgamation order. Such "interest in" or "rights against" refers to real and substantive rights, as opposed to rights that are only in form. A shareholder or creditor gets effected by an amalgamation order, if the value of his share gets depleted as a result of the amalgamation and if dividends that have been paid to him are likely to come down as a result of the amalgamation. Likewise, a creditor of a solvent company is directly effected by an amalgamation by which the amount loaned by such creditor becomes, as a result of the amalgamation, less likely to be paid back in time, than if the amalgamation did not take place. Such rights and interests of members and creditors are substantive rights which, when effected by the amalgamation, lead to compensation having to be paid. Every shareholder of a company and indeed, every creditor of a company, is concerned only with the "economic value" of his share or the loan granted to a company, as the case may be. The moment the share value, in real terms, is likely to dip, and/or loans granted are likely not to be repaid in time or at all as a result of an amalgamation, such members or creditors of the amalgamating company are equally entitled to be compensated for this economic loss as are the members and creditors of the amalgamated company, depending on the facts of each case. A reasonable construction must be given to Section 396. [65]

12. Thus, it is clear from a reading of Section 396(3), (3A), and (4)(aa) that, every member or creditor of each of the companies before amalgamation shall have, as nearly as may be, the same interest in or rights against the company resulting from the amalgamation as he had in the original company. To the extent to which the interest or rights of such member or creditor are less than his interest or rights against the original company, post amalgamation, he shall be entitled to compensation which is to be assessed. Post assessment, if such member or creditor is aggrieved, he may prefer an appeal to the appellate authority under Sub-section (3A). Under Sub-section (4)(aa), no order of amalgamation can be made unless

the time for preferring an appeal under Sub-section (3A) has expired, or where any such appeal has been preferred, the appeal has been finally disposed of. [66]

13. Fact that, the assessment order dated 1st April, 2015 did not provide any compensation to either the shareholders or creditors of FTIL for the economic loss caused by the amalgamation in breach of Section 396(3), it is clear that an important condition precedent to the passing of the final amalgamation order was not met. On this ground also, therefore, the final amalgamation order has to be held to be ultra vires Section 396 of the Companies Act, and, being arbitrary and unreasonable, violative of Article 14 of the Constitution of India. [74]

14. The order dated 12th February, 2016 is ultra vires Section 396 of the Companies Act, and violative of Article 14 of the Constitution. Appeals allowed. [76]

Disposition: Appeal Allowed

Collector of Ganjam and Ors. vs. Ramesh Chander Padhi (06.02.2009 - SC) : MANU/SC/0139/2009

Relative Section:

Essential Commodities Act, 1955 - Section 3, Section 6A, Section 6A(1), Section 6B, Section 6C, Section 6D, Section 7, Section 7(1)(6), Section 7(1)(a)

Hon'bleJudges/Coram:

Dr. Arijit Pasayat and A.K. Ganguly

Equivalent Citation: AIR2009SC1850, 2009(1)CLJ(SC)298, JT2009(3)SC511, 2009(II)OLR143, 2009(II)OLR(SC)143, 2009(2)RCR(Civil)352, 2009(2)RCR(Criminal)312, 2009(2)SCALE267, (2009) 17SCC492, (2011)1SCC(Cri)907, [2009]1SCR957, 2009(2)UJ614

Case Reference:

Deputy Commissioner, Dakshina Kannada District v. Rudolph Fernandes MANU/SC/0143/2000;

Shambhu Dayal Agarwala v. State of W.B. MANU/SC/0469/1990

NumberofPagesintheOriginalJudgment:5

Case Note:

Civil - Essential Commodities - Confiscation of vehicle - Imposition of fine - Section 6A(1) of the Essential Commodities Act, 1955 ("Act') - Scope of - Clause 8 of Orissa Kerosene Control Order, 1962 - Clause 3 of Kerosene Control (Restriction on use and Fixation of Ceiling Price) Order, 1993 - Proceedings were initiated for contravention of Clause 8 of Orissa Kerosene Control Order, 1962 read with Clause 3 of Kerosene Control (Restriction on use and Fixation of Ceiling Price), 1993 against the Respondent under Section 6A of the Act and directed confiscation of the vehicle - Collector in view of the provisions contained in Section 6A directed the Respondent to pay a fine of Rs. 20,000 - Hence, the present appeal - Petitioner contended that while considering the application for release of the vehicle, the Collector could not have concluded the proceedings under Section 6A(1) and even if the Collector concluded the proceedings under Section 6A(1), there was no reason for him to impose conditions such as payment of fine of Rs. 20,000 - Held, ratio in Deputy Commissioner, Dakshina Kannada District v. Rudolph Fernandes applied - Measure of fine which is required to be levied in lieu of confiscation under the second proviso to Section 6A(1) would be relatable to the market price of the vehicle and not of the seized essential commodity - And, the fine amount in lieu of confiscation is not to exceed the market price of the vehicle on the date of seizure of the essential commodity - Single Judge did not consider the scope and ambit of second proviso to Section 6A(1) of the Act in its proper perspective - Impugned order set aside - Matter remitted to the High Court - Appeal allowed.

Facts:

1. Facts leading to initiation of the aforesaid case is that on 21.12.2004 while the Marketing Inspector, Jaganathprasad Block, while following the Sub-Collector, Bhanjanagar during tour to Jaganathprasad Block, found one bus bearing registration No. OIG-185 parked at the Bus Stand and kerosene oil was being poured in the oil tank of the bus. Looking at them, both the driver and the conductor of the vehicle fled away. He drained out the kerosene oil from the oil tank of the bus which contained 42 liters of kerosene, and prepared the sample list by taking 2 liters out of the seized kerosene oil for its chemical examination. The bus as well as kerosene were seized and a proceeding bearing EME No. 37 of 2004 was initiated against the respondent and another under Section 6A of the Act. The proceeding was initiated for contravention of Clause 8 of Orissa Kerosene Control Order, 1962 read with Clause 3 of Kerosene Control (Restriction on use and Fixation of Ceiling Price), 1993. In the said proceeding, the respondent who is the owner of the bus filed an application for release of the vehicle. While deciding the aforesaid application, the Collector concluded the proceeding under Section 6A of the Act and directed confiscation of the vehicle. However, the Collector in view of the provisions contained in Section 6A of

the Act directed the respondent to pay a fine of Rs. 20,000/-.

Held by Hon'ble Court

1. As a matter of fact in Shambhu Dayal Agarwala's case (supra) (at para 6) this Court dealt with the position and observed as quoted .

In Shambhu Dayal Agarwala v. State of W.B. MANU/SC/0469/1990 : [1990]2SCR987 after considering the scheme of Sections 6A and 7 and dealing with the proviso (ii) to Sub-section (2) of Section 6A, this Court observed: (SCC p. 555, para 6)

Section 6A, therefore, merely confers power of confiscation and not the power of release, disposal, distribution, etc., except to the limited extent permitted by Sub-section (2) thereof. of course, the second proviso to Sub-section (1) of Section 6A permits the grant of an option to pay, in lieu of confiscation of any animal, vehicle, vessel or other conveyance, a fine equal to its market price at the date of seizure.

1. Learned Single Judge does not appear to have considered the scope and ambit of second proviso to Section 6A(1) of the Act in its proper perspective.
2. Accordingly, we set aside the impugned order and remit the matter to the High Court to consider the matter afresh in view of what has been stated in Deputy Commissioner, Dakshina's case (supra).
3. The appeal is allowed.

CHAPTER SIX

State of Bihar and Ors. vs. Arvind Kumar and Ors. (23.07.2012 - SC) : MANU/SC/0602/2012

Relative Section:

Code of Criminal Procedure, 1973 (CrPC) - Section 451; Section 457; Section 10, Section 3,

Section 6-A, Section 6-A(2), Section 6-C, Section 6-E, Section 7, Section 7(1), Section 7(1)(b); Indian Penal Code 1860, (IPC) - Section 421; Section 424.

Hon'bleJudges/Coram:

B.S. Chauhan and Swatanter Kumar

Equivalent Citation:2012ACR3548, 2012(118)AIC184, 2012 (79) ACC 396, 2012(3)BLJ220, III(2012) CCR269(SC), 2012(3)CLJ(SC)76, 2012CriLJ3756, 2013(1)ECrN 770, 2012(4)J.L.J.R.336, 2012(3) JCC2007(SC),JT2012(7)SC27,2012(4)PLJR233,2012(4)RCR(Criminal)209, 2012(6)SCALE61,(2012)12SCC395, [2012] 7SCR117, 2012(3)UC1673

Case Reference:

Shambhu Dayal Agarwala v. State of West Bengal and Anr. MANU/SC/0469/1990 : (1990) 3 SCC 549;

Oma Ram v. State of Rajasthan and Ors. MANU/SC/1852/2008 : (2008) 5 SCC 502;

Manish Goel v. Rohini Goel MANU/SC/0106/2010 : AIR 2010 SC 1099;

Vice Chancellor, University of Allahabad and Ors. v. Dr. Anand Prakash Mishra and Ors.

MANU/SC / 1486 / 1997 : (1997) 10 SCC 264;

Karnataka State Road Transport Corporation v. Ashrafulla Khan and Ors. MANU/SC/0022/2002 : AIR 2002 SC 629

NumberofPagesintheOriginalJudgment: 5

Case Note:

Criminal - Release of seized articles - Sections 3, 6-A and 6-C of Essential Commodities Act, 1955 - High Court held that continuing seizure of seized articles of Respondents by Appellant for long time might not be justified and therefore High Court issued direction for release of wheat - Hence, this Appeals - Whether, order passed by High Court was justified - Held, High Court had not even taken prima facie view that State Government had not issued twice any order/notification under Section 3 of Act though FIR made reference to Clause 6(a) of Public Distribution System (Control) Order, 2001 issued under Section 3 of Act - Further, there was nothing on record on basis of which issue of ownership had been decided by High Court - There was no cogent material on record before High Court on basis of which direction to release goods so seized could be issued - In subsequent order dealing with ownership of wheat High Court had only taken note of fact that as Respondents were prepared to furnish adequate/sufficient security to satisfaction of Court below for release of wheat in question, wheat could have been released by CJM - In case CJM came to conclusion after appreciating evidence on record that Respondents/Applicants were not in position to show any document which may show their ownership to wheat, there was no justification for High Court to issue directions for release of such material merely because Applicant could furnish security - High Court had ignored fact that any order passed under Section 6-A of Act was appealable under Section 6-C of Act - Hence, order passed by High Court was not justified - Appeals disposed of.

Ratio Decidendi:

"No Court has competence to issue direction contrary to law nor shall Court direct an Authority to act in contravention of statutory provisions."

Facts:

Facts and circumstances giving rise to these appeals are that:

A. On 15.2.2011, a secret information was received by the department of the Appellants in respect of illegal storage of subsidized food grains of Public Distribution Scheme by the Respondents which led to the raid upon the premises of M/s Harsh Tejas Nutrition Pvt. Ltd., (Flour Mill of the Respondents) situate at Patna, New Bypass Road near Petrol Pump.

The Sub-Divisional Officer, Patna City and other officers from the local police raided the premises of the said flour mill and found off loading of wheat from Truck bearing registration No. BHI 1899. The driver and other workers fled away. It was found that the grains bags had the seal of Food Corporation of India, (hereinafter called `FCI'), U.P. Government Food Department, Food and Supply Department, Haryana; and Government of Punjab. The seized material made it apparent that there had been diversion of FCI grains for the purpose of black marketing. Appellants seized 5923 bags filled with more than 2991 quintals wheat.

B. None from the company where the raid was conducted came forward to claim the seized material or to justify the storage of same. Thus, the FIR bearing case No. 15/2011 dated 18.2.2011 was lodged under Sections 7 and 10 of the EC Act in addition to the appropriate Sections 421/424 of the Indian Penal Code, 1860 (hereinafter called 'Indian Penal Code') in respect of the said seizure.

C. The Respondents herein preferred Criminal Writ Petition No. 215/ 2011 for quashing confiscation proceedings and/or release of the confiscated goods.

D. The High Court allowed the said writ petition within a very short span vide order dated 15.3.2011 and subject to certain procedural compliances observed that continuing seizure of the seized articles for a long time may not be justified and therefore the High Court issued direction for release of the said wheat.

E. The Respondent approached the Chief Judicial Magistrate, Patna, for releasing the wheat in pursuance of the order passed by the High Court on 15.3.2011 by moving an application. The learned CJM dismissed the application of the Respondent on 7.4.2011 on the ground that he could not produce any document which may show their ownership to the said seized material.

F. The Respondent again approached the High Court by filing Criminal Miscellaneous No. 14692/2011 which had been allowed vide order dated 29.4.2011.

Hence, these appeals.

Held by Hon'ble Court

10. What we found shocking in the instant case is that the petition was filed before the High Court for quashing of the FIR and alternatively for releasing the seized items and the High Court without giving any reason whatsoever disposed of the petition observing as under:

Considering the submissions of the parties, in the opinion of the court, continuing the seizure of the seized items for a long time may not be justified at least the seizure of the wheat.

This is the only reason given by the High Court without even considering what were the averments on behalf of the parties and without considering the requirement of the statutory provisions.

11. In the subsequent order dealing with the ownership of the wheat the High Court has only taken note of the fact that as the Respondents herein were prepared to furnish adequate/sufficient security to the satisfaction of the court below for release of the wheat in question, the wheat could have been released by the CJM. In case the learned CJM came to the conclusion after appreciating the evidence on record that the Respondents/applicants were not in a position to show any document which may show their ownership to the wheat, there was no justification for the High Court to issue directions for release of such material merely because applicant could furnish the security.

If it is so, any stranger or third party may give sufficient security and get the seized goods release in his favour. Such a course is not permissible even while deciding the application under Section 451/457 of the Code of Criminal Procedure, 1973. A person having no title/ownership over the seized material may get the same released on furnishing security and sell it in black market and earn profit several times more than the amount of security furnished by him. We fail to understand as how such an order of release which defeat the very purpose for which the EC Act was enacted, could be passed.

12. The High Court has totally ignored the fact that any order passed under Section 6-A is appealable under Section 6-C of the EC Act. Therefore, to consider such an application for release of the goods was totally unwarranted at least at that stage.

13. In Manish Goel v. Rohini Goel MANU/SC/0106/2010 : AIR 2010 SC 1099, this Court has held that generally, no Court has competence to issue a direction contrary to law nor the Court can direct an authority to act in contravention of the statutory provisions. The courts are meant to enforce the rule of law and not to pass the orders or directions which are contrary to what has been injected by law. (See also: Vice Chancellor, University of Allahabad and Ors. v. Dr. Anand Prakash Mishra and Ors. MANU/SC/1486/1997 : (1997) 10 SCC 264; and Karnataka State Road Transport Corporation v. Ashrafulla Khan and Ors. MANU/SC/0022/2002

: AIR 2002 SC 629).

14. Learned Counsel for the parties are not in a position to reveal the status of the criminal proceedings initiated against the Respondents. In such a fact-situation, as has been suggested by Learned Counsel for the parties we set aside the aforesaid judgments and orders dated 15.3.2011 and 29.4.2011 and remand the case back to the High Court to consider afresh after examining all factual and legal issues involved in the case. Till the disposal of the case afresh, interim order passed by this Court on 31.10.2011 shall remain operative.

The appeals stand disposed of accordingly.

CHAPTER SEVEN

S. Samuel and Ors. vs. Union of India (UOI) and Ors. (06.11.2003 - SC) : MANU/SC/0892/2003

Relative Section:

Drugs And Cosmetics Act, 1940 - Section 3; Essential Commodities Act, 1955 - Section 2, Section 2(xi), Section 3, Section 3(1), Section 3(a), Section 5; Tea Act, 1953 - Section 2

Hon'bleJudges/Coram:

R.C. Lahoti and Ashok Bhan

Equivalent Citation: 004(13)AIC307, 2004(2)ALT8(SC), JT2003(8)SC413, 2004-2-LW(Crl)690, 2004(2)PLJR120, 2004(1)RCR(Civil)188, 2003(9)SCALE442, (2004)1SCC256, [2003]Supp5SCR295, [2003]134STC610(SC)

Case Reference:

Hinde v. Allmond, (1918) 87 LJKB 893;

The State of Bombay v. Virkumar Gulabchand Shah, MANU/SC/0005/1952;

K. Janardhan Pillai and Anr. v. Union of India and Ors., MANU/SC/0021/1981;

Collector of Central Excise, Bombay-I and Anr. v. Parle Exports (P) Ltd., MANU/SC/0081/1988;

Brooke Bond (India) Limited v. Union of India, MANU/AP/0046/1980

NumberofPagesintheOriginalJudgment: 12

Case Note:

Constitution -Tamil Nadu Scheduled Articles (Prescription of Standards) Order, 1977; Essential Commodities Act, 1955 - Sections 2, 3, 3(1), 3(2) and 5; Drugs and Cosmetics Act, 1940 - Section 3; Tea Act, 1953 - Section 2; Food Hoarding Order, 1917 -Constitutional validity of the Tamil Nadu Scheduled Articles (Prescription of Standards) order, 1977 - Parliament can issue notification in respect of that commodity with respect to which the Parliament has power to make laws by virtue of Entry 33 in List III in the Seventh Schedule of the Constitution - Food' may include not only solid substances but also a drink - Whether a solid or a liquid, the substance called 'food' should possess the quality to maintain life and its growth; it must have nutritive or nourishing value so as to enable the growth, repair or maintenance of the body - The Central Government has declared the commodity 'tea' to be an essential commodity - With effect from the date of the said Notification, tea becomes an essential commodity by reference to the power exercised by the Central Government under Section 2(xi) of the Essential Commodity Act read with Entry 33 in List III in the Seventh Schedule to the Constitution and Section 2 of the Tea Act, 1953 - No delegation of powers by the Central Government under Section 5 of the Essential Commodity Act in relation to tea. - State of Tamil Nadu could not have promulgated an order under Section 3 of the Essential Commodity Act in the purported exercise of the power delegated by the Central Government to make an order applicable to tea, by wrongly assuming tea to be a foodstuff, the several provisions of the Tamil Nadu Scheduled Articles (Prescription of Standards) Order, 1977, must be held to be ultra vires the power of the State Government to the extent to which it makes provisions in relation to tea - The said order cannot apply to tea - Appeal Allowed

Facts:

1. Challenge to the constitutional validity of the Tamil Nadu Scheduled Articles (Prescription of Standards) order, 1977 (hereinafter referred to as the Order, for short) in its application to 'tea' having failed, the appellants are in appeal by special leave. The crux of the controversy centers around the question whether 'tea' can be included within the meaning of 'foodstuffs' listed as Sub-clause (v) of Clause (a) of Section 2 of the Essential commodities act, 1955 (hereinafter, the EC Act, for short) which defines "essential commodity".

2. The EC Act was enacted to provide, in the Interest of the general public, for the control of the production, supply and distribution of and

trade and commerce, in certain commodities. The phrase 'essential commodity' is defined by Clause (a) of Section 2 of the EC Act as under:

Held by Hon'ble Court

1. A perusal of the judgment of the High Court shows that the Division Bench was of the opinion, as recorded vide para 16 of the impugned Judgment, that - In this country it is too well known that many a poor man who live under the poverty line take a cup of tea more as a food as it keeps them active for some time and enables them to work. We cannot agree. It is a wrong assumption to say that many a poor man in the country take a cup of tea more as a food. The High Court has confused a mere stimulant with an article of food or foodstuffs. We have already dealt with in detail the issue that. 3 drink or beverage which acts merely as a stimulant is not food.

2. As we have held that the State of Tamil Nadu could not have promulgated an order under Section 3 of the E.C. Act in the purported exercise of the power delegated by the Central Government to make an order applicable to tea, by wrongly assuming tea to be a foodstuff, the several provisions of the Tamil Nadu Scheduled Articles (Prescription of Standards) Order, 1977, must be held to be ultra vires the power of the State Government to the extent to which it makes provisions in relation to tea. The said order cannot apply to tea.

2. In view of the above said finding, it is not necessary to deal with the other contention raised on behalf of the appellant viz, that the order is invalid and ineffective as it is not accompanied by the previous concurrence of the Central Government.

4. The appeals are allowed. The impugned judgment of the High Court is set aside. The writ petition, filed by the appellants as writ petitioners in the High Court, shall stand allowed.

CHAPTER EIGHT

Deputy Commissioner, Dakshina Kannada District vs. Rudolph Fernandes (29.02.2000 - SC) : MANU/ SC/0143/2000

Relative Section:

Customs Act, 1962 - Section 115(2);

Essential Commodities Act, 1955 - Section 3, Section 5, Section 6A,Section 6A(1), Section 6B, Section 6B(2), Section 6C,Section 6D, Section 7,Section 7(1),Section 7(1)(a)

Hon'bleJudges/Coram:

B.N. Kirpal and M.B. Shah

Equivalent Citation: AIR2000SC1132, 2001 (Suppl.) ACC 17, 2000 (39) ALR 252, 2000(4)ALT21(SC), 2000 (2) AWC 1305 (SC), 2000(2)BLJ604, JT2000(2)SC508, 2000-2-LW(Crl)733, 2000(2)RCR(Civil)512, RLW2000(1)SC141, 2000(2)SCALE172, (2000)3SCC306, [2000]2SCR24

Case Reference:

Shambhu Dayal Agarwala v. State of West Bengal and Another MANU/ SC/0469/1990

NumberofPagesintheOriginalJudgment:5

Case Note:

Commercial - seizure - Section 3, 6A (1) and 7 of Essential Commodities Act, 1955 - whether fine imposed in lieu of confiscation should be market price of essential commodity seizcd - fine imposed in lieu of confiscation should be related to market price of vehicle seized on date of seizure of essential commodity - fine should not exceed market price of vehicle seized.

Facts:

C. A. No. 3214 of 1989.

1. In this appeal, a Matador (Mini Lorry) carrying 44 bags of cement was intercepted and seized by the Bajpe Police, Dakshina Kartnada on 22-8-1983. Proceedings under Section 6A of the Act were initiated before the Deputy Commissioner. During the pendency of the proceedings, the respondent applied for interim release of vehicle and the same was granted by order dated 1-9-1983 on his furnishing a bank guarantee of Rs. one lakh. That, order was challenged by the respondent before the High Court of Karnataka at Bangalore In W.P. No. 166G8 of 1983 on the ground that imposition of such condition was illegal and onerous. The learned Single Judge after considering second proviso to Section 6A(1) held that the words "market price" occurring in the section relate only to "the essential commodity sought to be carried". According to the learned Judge "the proviso gives a concession to the owner to avert confiscation by paying fine not exceeding the market price prevalent on the date of its seizure of the essential commodity". According to the learned Judge if option is to pay a fine equivalent to the market price of the vehicle then there is no necessity to give such option. Owner instead of paying a fine equivalent to the market price can as well think of purchasing a new or fresh vehicle. He, there fore, directed release of the vehicle accepting the Bank Guarantee to the extent of Rs. 500/- only. Being aggrieved the State preferred an appeal before the Division Bench of the High Court in WA No. 2248 of 1983 which was also dismissed by the impugned order dated 22-3-1988.

C.A. Nos. 5074-75 of 1989

2. In these appeals, two transport vehicles belonging to the respondents carrying paddy were seized by the Police for the alleged contravention of Food Control Orders. Applications were filed before the Deputy Commissioner for release of said vehicles. By order dated 16-2-1989 the Deputy Commissioner passed an order directing the release of the vehicles in question on their furnishing Bank Guarantee in a sum of Rupees three lakhs each. That order was challenged before the High Court of Karnataka by filing Writ Petitions Nos. 3563 and 3579 of 1989. The High Court following its earlier decision in Rudolph Fernandes v. Deputy Commissioner, D.K. MANU/KA/0184/1984 : AIR1984Kant106 (C.A. No.

3214/89 before us) allowed the writ petitions and reduced the fine amount to rupees 10,000/-each.

3. Both the orders are challenged before us in these appeals.

4. The short question involved in these appeals is - whether fine in lieu of confiscation contemplated under the second proviso to Section 6A(1) of the Essential Commodities Act, 1955 (hereinafter referred to as "The Act') provides for levy of fine on the basis of market value of the confiscated vehicle or on the basis of the market price of the essential commodity sought to be carried by such vehicle. Section 6A of the Act is as under:

Held by Hon'ble Court

1. The Court observed that though the language of the aforesaid proviso is clear, the idea sought to be conveyed under the proviso to Section 6A(1) of the Act appear to be the same. In our view, the analogy drawn by the High Court is erroneous because the proviso specifically mentions that where any such conveyance is used as a means of transport in the smuggling of goods, the owner of any conveyance is to be given an option to pay in lieu of the confiscation of the conveyance, a fine not exceeding the market price of the goods which are sought to be smuggled. Explanation provides that market price means market price at the date when the goods are seized. As against this, Section 6A second proviso does not refer to payment of fine not exceeding market price of the essential commodity but apparent reference is a fine not exceeding the market price of the vehicle sought to be confiscated. This appears to be obvious because in case where market price of the seized essential commodity is more than the price of the conveyance then owner of the conveyance would not come forward to take it back if he is asked to pay something more than its market price. Similarly, when the market price of the seized vehicle is much more than of the essential commodity, it cannot be said that instead of confiscation it should be released at a price which is less than its market price. Further it is required to be noted that under Section 6B(2) no order confiscating vehicle or other conveyance can be passed if the owner proves to the satisfaction of the competent authority that it was used in carrying the essential commodity without his knowledge or connivance.

2. In the result, the appeals are allowed and the impugned orders holding that measure of imposing fine in lieu of confiscation under second proviso to Section 6A of the Essential Commodities Act would be the market price of the essential commodity seized are set aside. However, considering the fact that since vehicles are already released, no further directions are

required to be given with regard to the fine amount in lieu of confiscation.

3. Order accordingly. No costs.

• 39 •

Union of India (UOI) vs. Ranbaxy Laboratories Ltd. and Ors. (12.05.2008 - SC) : MANU/SC/7677/2008

Relative Section:

Essential Commodities Act, 1955 - Section 10, Section 3, Section 3(2)(c),Section 7A

Hon'bleJudges/Coram:

S.B. Sinha and V.S. Sirpurkar

Equivalent Citation: AIR2008SC2286, 2008 (4) AWC 3490 (SC), 2008 (3) CCC 149 , 3(2008)CLT470, JT2008(6)SC647, (2008)7SCC502

Case Reference:

Union of India v. Cynamide India Ltd. MANU/SC/0076/1987;

Prag Ince and Oil Mills v. Union of India MANU/SC/0493/1978;

Sree Meenakshi Mills v. Union of India MANU/SC/0058/1972;

New India Assurance Co. Ltd. v. Nusli Neville Wadia and Anr. MANU/SC/0166/2008;

Oriental Insurance Co. Ltd. v. Brij Mohan and Ors. MANU/SC/7682/2007

NumberofPagesintheOriginalJudgment: 7

Case Note:

(1) Essential Commodities Act, 1955 - Sections 2 (a), 2 (s) and 10--Drugs Price (Control) Order, 1995--Paras 23 and 25--Bulk drug including Pentazocine--Exemption under Control Order--Granted to first respondent--Expired on 31.10.1999 --Whether drug manufactured upto

31.10.1999 could be sold on and from 1.11.1999 at price specified in order as exemption not available?--Held, "no"--If first respondent entitled to avail benefit of exemption notification till midnight of 31.10.1999--Some time would be necessary for it to market same--There must be some time lag between period during which drug manufactured--And actual sale by retail dealer to customer--Drug manufactured on 31.10.1999--Cannot be sold on same day--No merit in appeal.

(2) Exemption notification--Interpretation -- While construing exemption notification--Not only pragmatic view required to be taken--But also practical aspect of it.

Ratio Decidendi: "Any exemption notification must be construe by keeping in view the practical aspects

Facts:

1. First respondent is a pharmaceutical company and is engaged in the manufacture, inter alia, of the bulk drug Pentazocine in the formulation of Pentazocine injection with the brand name `Fortwin'. Sale and marketing of the said drug is controlled by the Drugs (Price Control) Order, 1995 (1995 Order). The said order has been made by the Central Government in exercise of its powers under Section 3 of the Essential Commodities Act, 1955 (1955 Act). We may notice some interpretation clauses in the 1955 Act, which are as under:

2.(a) "bulk drug" means any pharmaceutical, chemical, biological or plant product including its salts, esters, stereo-isomers and derivatives, conforming to pharmacopoeial or other standards specified in the Second Schedule to the Drugs and Cosmetics Act, 1940 (23 of 1940), and which is used as such or as an ingredient in any formulation;

2. The exemption granted in favour of the first respondent had expired on 31st October, 1999.

3. First respondent was asked to show cause as to why an amount of Rs. 2,59,76,070/- should not be recovered from it and why action should not be taken under paragraphs 21 and 24 of 1995 Order read with Section 10 of the 1955 Act by a notice dated 29th April, 2002. In response thereto the first respondent inter alia contended that it had not overcharged price from any customer and no amount towards any alleged over charge was payable by it. It was furthermore contended that the company had furnished all the informations, as and when asked for by the prescribed authorities of the appellant.

4. As the said reply was found to be unsatisfactory, the first respondent was asked to deposit the alleged over charged amount with interest @ 15% per annum as provided under Section 7A of the 1955 Act.

5. A writ petition was filed there against by the first respondent before the Delhi High Court. The said writ petition was dismissed by a learned Single Judge of the said High Court by an order dated 20th May, 2004.

6. A Letters Patent Appeal was filed there against which has been allowed by a Division Bench of the said Court by reason of the impugned judgment and order dated 19th December, 2005.

Held by Hon'ble Court

While referring to its decision in Oriental Insurance Co. Ltd. v. Brij Mohan and Ors. MANU/SC/7682/2007 : AIR2007SC1971 it applied the doctrine of purposive construction. Applying the principle of doctrine of purposive construction, we are of the opinion that meaningful purpose could be achieved only if the construction of the notification as indicated hereinbefore is adopted and no other.

There is no merit in this appeal which fails and is accordingly dismissed with costs. Counsel's fee assessed at Rs. 50,000/-.

Harendra Nath Chakraborty vs. State of West Bengal (19.12.2008 - SC) : MANU/ SC/8450/2008

Relative Section:

Code of Criminal Procedure, 1973 (CrPC) - Section 313; Section 360; Section 2A, Section 3, Section 7(1), Section 7(1)(a)(ii);

Indian Evidence Act, 1872 - Section 114(g);

Indian Penal Code 1860, (IPC) - Section 302

Hon'ble Judges/**Coram:**

S.B. Sinha and Cyriac Joseph, JJ.

Equivalent Citation: 2009(76)AIC153, 2009(1)ALD(Cri)499, 2009 (65) ACC 152, I(2009)CCR210(SC), CLT(2009)Supp.Crl.16, 2009(1)CTC399, 2009(1)JKJ50[SC], 2009(1)RCR(Criminal)660, 2009(1)SCALE399, (2009)2SCC758

Case Reference:

State of Punjab v. Swaran Singh MANU/SC/0427/2005;

Mr. Rauf Rahim on Vikramjit Singh Alias Vicky v. State of Punjab (2006) 12 SCC 306; Harivallabha and Anr. v. State of M.P. (2005) 10 SCC 330;

State of Punjab v. Prem Sagar and Ors. MANU/SC/7692/2008

NumberofPagesintheOriginalJudgment:8

Case Note:

Criminal - Conviction - Section 7(1) (a) (ii) of Essential Commodities Act, 1955 - Single Judge of High Court convicted Appellant for an offence punishable under Section 7(1)(a)(ii) of Act - Hence, this Appeal - Whether,

conviction of Appellant was erroneous - Held, prosecution case was purely
based on documentary evidence maintained by accused himself - Where
e prosecution intends to bring home charges on basis of the documentary
evidence maintained by accused himself, it could not be equated with a
case where accused was charged with commission of an offence - However,
said provision could be invoked provided Court was in a position to assign
special reasons - Moreover, no case had been made out to invoke proviso
appended to Section 7(1)(a)(ii) of Act particularly in view of fact that
Appellant was found to have violated provisions of both Orders - Therefore,
if Parliament had provided for a minimum sentence, same should ordinarily
be imposed save and except some exceptional cases which might justified
invocation of proviso appended thereto - Thus, High Court had taken into
consideration entire facts and circumstances and reduced period of
imprisonment from six months to three months - Hence, Appellant should
surrender before Special Judge for serving out remaining sentence - Appeal
allowed.

Ratio Decidendi:

"Courts shall exercise their power judicially and relief granted by them
shall be logical and tenable within framework of law."

Facts:

1. Appellant was a dealer in kerosene oil having been granted licence in
terms of the provisions of the West Bengal Kerosene Control Order, 1968
(for short, "the 1968 Order") made by the State of West Bengal in exercise
of its powers conferred by Sub-section (1) of Section 3 of the Act read with
clauses (d), (e), (h) and (j) of Sub-section (2) of that Section and Section
7(1) thereof as also the Order No. 26(11)-Com.Genl/66, dated 18th June,
1966.

2. The State of West Bengal apart from the aforementioned 1968 Order
made West Bengal Declaration of Stocks and Prices of Essential
Commodities Order, 1977 (for short, "the 1977 Order")

3. Indisputably, kerosene is an essential commodity within the meaning
of Sub-section (1) of Section 2A of the Act. For dealing in the said
commodity, a licence is required to be taken under the 1968 Order.
Appellant was holder of a licence bearing No. DP/64 in terms whereof he
was entitled to deal in the said commodity.

4. Section 7(1)(a)(ii) provides for imposition of a penalty on a person
who contravenes any order made under Section 3 with imprisonment for
a term which shall not be less than three months but which may extend to

seven years and shall also be liable to fine. The proviso appended thereto postulates that the court may, for any adequate and special reasons to be recorded in the judgment, impose a sentence of imprisonment for a term of less than three months.

5. Manik Lal Das, a Sub-Inspector of Police conducted a raid in the shop of the appellant on 28.1.1991. Several irregularities were found. A first information report was lodged inter alia alleging:

Held by Hon'ble Court

1. In the facts and circumstances of the case, we are of the opinion that no case has been made out to invoke the proviso appended to Section 7(1)(a)(ii) of the Act particularly in view of the fact that appellant was found to have violated the provisions of both the Orders.

2. Appellant was dealing with an essential commodity like kerosene.

3. If the Parliament has provided for a minimum sentence, the same should ordinarily be imposed save and except some exceptional cases which may justify invocation of the proviso appended thereto.

4. In India, we do not have any statutory sentencing policy as has been noticed by this Court in State of Punjab v. Prem Sagar and Ors. MANU/SC/7692/2008 : 2008CriLJ3533 . Ordinarily, the legislative sentencing policy as laid in some special Acts where the Parliamentary intent has been expressed in unequivocal terms should be applied. Sentence of less than the minimum period prescribed by the Parliament may be imposed only in exceptional cases. No such case has been made out herein.

5. For the reasons aforementioned, the appeal is dismissed. Appellant shall surrender before the learned Special Judge for serving out the remaining sentence.

CHAPTER ELEVEN

Kailash Prasad Yadav and Ors. vs. State of Jharkhand and Ors. (02.05.2007 - SC) : MANU/SC/7602/2007

Relative Section:

Essential Commodities Act, 1955 - Section 3, Section 6A, Section 6A(1)

Hon'bleJudges/Coram:

S.B. Sinha and Markandey Katju

Equivalent Citation: 2007(3)ACR2499(SC), 2007(54)AIC24, AIR2007SC2626, 2007 (58) ACC 563, 2007(2)ALT(Cri)153, 2007(6)ALT6(SC), 2007(2)BLJ52, II(2007)CCR493(SC), 2007CriLJ3722, JT2007(6)SC369, 2007(II)OLR471, 2007(II)OLR(SC)471, 2007(4)RCR(Criminal)24, 2007(6)SCALE461, (2007)5SCC769, [2007]5SCR1150

Case Reference:

Shambhu Dayal Agarwala v. State of West Bengal and Anr. MANU/SC/ 0469/1990;

Deputy Commissioner, Dakshina Kannada District v. Rudolph Fernandes MANU/SC/0143/2000

NumberofPagesintheOriginalJudgment:4

Case Note:

Essential Commodities Act, 1955 - Sections 3 and 6A (1) (c)--Confiscation of truck--Violation of order under Section 3--Is pre-condition for passing order of confiscation -- Public Distribution System (Control) Order, 2001 does not contain any provision for search of vehicle--Valid

seizure is sine qua non for passing order of confiscation of property--
Vehicle allegedly carrying wheat belonging to F.C.I.--Order of confiscation
is not passed mere because it would be lawful to do so--Authorities must
arrive at clear finding that there was violation of Section 3 -- On facts and
circumstances of case not fit case where order of confiscation could have
been passed--Impugned judgments unsustainable and set aside.

Ratio Decidendi :

Confiscation of vehicles - Violation of provisions of Act - Order of
confiscation can only be passed after authorities arrived at a clear finding in
regard to violation made under Section 3 - Order of confiscation cannot not
be passed when the matter was pending before the Criminal Court

Facts:

1. Appellants were owners of a truck. The said truck was hired for
transportation of foodgrains by one Kailash Chand Sahu. It was allegedly
carrying wheat belonging to the Food Corporation of India. A confiscation
proceeding was initiated. An order of confiscation was passed by the
Deputy Commissioner, Sahibganj. An appeal preferred there against has
been dismissed by the Additional Sessions Judge I, Sahibganj by an order
dated 7.03.2005 passed in Criminal (Confiscation) Appeal No. 32 of 2003.
Appellants filed a writ petition before the Jharkhand High Court which by
reason of the impugned judgment has been dismissed by a learned Single
Judge of the said Court.

2. Mr. H.L. Agrawal, learned senior counsel appearing on behalf of the
appellants, in support of this appeal, would submit that wheat being a de-
controlled item and there being no control whatsoever, either on trading
of wheat or possession or transportation thereof, the impugned judgment
cannot be sustained.

3. Mr. B.B. Singh, learned Counsel appearing on behalf of the State, on
the other, would submit that the appellants having abetted a fair price shop
dealer who was appointed under the Public Distribution System (Control)
Order, 2001 (for short "the 2001 Order", the impugned order cannot be
faulted with.

Held by Hon'ble Court

1. We have to consider the matter from another angle. The order of
confiscation is not passed only because it would be lawful to do so. The
authorities must arrive at a clear finding in regard to the violation made
under Section 3 of the Act. The issues which have been raised before us
have not been considered either by the Deputy Commissioner or by the

learned Sessions Judge as also by the High Court. The matter is pending before the criminal court. We, therefore, do not intend to delve further into the matter. Keeping in view the facts and circumstances of this case, we are of the opinion that it was not a fit case where an order of confiscation could have been passed.

11. Reliance placed by Mr. Singh on Shambhu Dayal Agarwala v. State of West Bengal and Anr. MANU/SC/0469/1990 : [1990]2SCR987 , itself stated the law, thus:

2. Section 6A empowers confiscation of the seized essential commodity, the package, covering and receptacle in which the essential commodity was found and the animal, vehicle or other conveyance in which such essential commodity was carried. The words 'may order confiscation' convey that the power is discretionary and not obligatory

3. Yet again, in Deputy Commissioner, Dakshina Kannada District v. Rudolph Fernandes MANU/SC/0143/2000 : [2000]2SCR24 , whereupon again Mr. Singh has relied upon, it was held:

In the light of the aforesaid provisions, the second proviso to Section 6A [sic 6A(1)] is required to be considered. First it is to be stated that the proviso limits the power of the competent authority to recover fine up to the market price for releasing the animal, vehicle, vessel or other conveyance sought to be confiscated. So maximum fine that can be levied in lieu of confiscation should not exceed the market price. For our purpose, the relevant part of the proviso would be "in the case of...vehicle...the owner of such...vehicle...shall be given an option to pay, in lieu of its confiscation, a fine not exceeding the market price at the date of seizure of the essential commodity sought to be carried by such...vehicle". Question is whether fine should not exceed the market price of the seized essential commodity or whether it should not exceed the market price of the vehicle. For this purpose, it appears that there is some ambiguity in the section. It is not specifically provided that in lieu of confiscation of the vehicle a fine not exceeding the market price of the vehicle or of the seized essential commodity is to be taken as a measure. Still however, it is difficult to say that the measure of fine is related to the market price of the essential commodity at the date of its seizure. It nowhere provides that fine should not exceed the market price of the essential commodity at the date of seizure of the vehicle. The proviso requires the competent authority to give an option to the owner of such vehicle to pay in lieu of confiscation a fine not exceeding the market price. What is to be confiscated is the vehicle and, therefore, the measure of fine would be relatable to the market price of the vehicle at the date of seizure of the essential commodity sought to be carried by such vehicle....

4. We do not intend to deal with the question as to whether upon conclusion of the trial, a case for forfeiture of the vehicle may be passed or not, being wholly irrelevant at this stage.

5.For the reasons aforementioned, the impugned judgments cannot be sustained, which are set aside accordingly. The appeal is allowed.

CHAPTER TWELVE

Duncan Industries Ltd. and Ors. vs. Union of India (UOI) (10.02.2006 - SC) : MANU/SC/0908/2006

Relative Section:

Constitution Of India - Article 14; Essential Commodities Act, 1955 - Section 3

Hon'bleJudges/Coram:

H.K. Sema and B.N. Srikrishna

Equivalent Citation: AIR2006SC3699, 2006 (2) AWC 1162 (SC), 2006(1)JKJ42[SC], JT2006(2)SC294, 2006(2)SCALE284, (2006)3SCC129

Case Reference:

Neyveli Lignite Corporation Ltd. v. Commercial Tax Officer MANU/SC/0599/2001; Associated Provincial Picture Houses Ltd. v. Wednesbury Corporation [1948] 1 KB 223;

BALCO Employees' Union (Regd) v. Union of India, MANU/SC/0779/2001;

Bhavesh D. Parish v. Union of India MANU/SC/0392/2000;

Peerless General Finance and Investment Co. Ltd. v. Reserve Bank of India MANU/SC/0685/1992;

State of M.P. v. Nandlal Jaiswal MANU/SC/0034/1986;

Premji Bhai Parmar v. Delhi Development Authority MANU/SC/0422/1979;

Noble State Bank v. IIaskell 219 US 575

NumberofPagesintheOriginalJudgment:11

Case Note:

Constitution of India - Article 14--Essential Commodities Act, 1955--Section 3--Fertilizer (Control) Order, 1957 -- Clause 3--Arbitrariness--Legitimate expectation --Fertilizer subsidies known as "Retention Price Scheme" (Scheme) granted by Central Government--Introduction of scheme in nitrogenous fertilizer industry w.e.f. 1.11.1977--In 2000-01 complaints voiced that fertilizer manufacturers misusing scheme--Whether scheme could be modified retrospectively to detriment of appellant manufacturers?--Held, "yes"--This scheme is mere administrative without any statutory flavour--Scheme has always had element of retrospectivity built-in--Undertaking entered into by manufacturers clearly allows Government to retrospectively revise pricing norms/policy for scheme--Scheme grounded on agreement between Government and certain fertilizer manufacturers--Hence, scheme not compulsorily imposed on fertilizer manufacturers -- No assurance actually breached by Government--Nothing arbitrary or unreasonable in what F.I.C. Committee has done--Scheme being voluntary--Doctrine of 'legitimate expectation' has no application--Article 14 does not require Supreme Court to examine intricacies of economic scheme or pricing policy for its merits or correctness--No merit in appeals.

Facts:

1. M/s Duncan Industries Ltd. (hereinafter "the First Appellant") is engaged in the business of manufacturing and selling urea (a fertilizer). In 1993, the First Appellant acquired the urea plant of M/'s Indian Explosives Ltd. (a unit of ICI India Ltd.). The Second Appellant is a shareholder in the First Appellant-Company (hereinafter, collectively "the appellants").

2. A Civil Miscellaneous Writ Petition No. 43934/2001 was moved by the appellants in the High Court of Judicature at Allahabad to challenge the interim revision of Retention Price made on 5.11.2001 and the consequent demand raised upon the First Appellant on 13.11.2001 for recovery of Rs. 184.01 crores under the Scheme. Although, the appellants had filed the Writ Petition sometime in 2001, it was actually moved in 2002, by which time the Government had recovered Rs. 127.21 crores by way of adjustments, leaving a balance of Rs. 56.80 crores.

3. A Civil Miscellaneous Application No. 40383/2002 was taken out by the appellants for interim relief which was disposed of by an agreed order. A perusal of the agreed order made on 3.4.2002 does not indicate that there was any challenge to the manner of computation of the Retention Price, but only suggested that the recovery of the balance amount of Rs. 56.80 crores

be made in 10 monthly installments, subject to disposal of a representation made by the appellants. On the question of payment of subsidy for the month of January 2002, it was stated in the order itself that it would be subject to the Government's power of revision, review and recovery of excess payment, if exercised, in the future.

4. The appellants challenged the working of the Retention Price Scheme by Civil Miscellaneous Writ Petition No. 43042/2002. This Writ Petition was dismissed by the High Court through the impugned judgment dated 7.11.2003. By another order dated 7.11.2003, following the impugned judgment, the High Court also dismissed Civil Miscellaneous Writ Petition No. 43934/2001.

Held by Hon'ble Court

Despite the bulky material and lengthy arguments presented to us, we find that this is a case full of sound and fury, signifying nothing. Indeed, we have found against the appellants on every point that they have chosen to impugn the judgment of the High Court. In the result, these appeals must fail and are hereby dismissed with no order as to costs.

CHAPTER THIRTEEN

Tarak Nath Keshari vs. State of West Bengal (10.05.2023 - SC) : MANU/SC/0558/2023

Relative Section:

Essential Commodities Act, 1955 - Section 3, Section 7, Section 7(1); Probation Of Offenders Act, 1958 - Section 4

Hon'ble Judges/Coram:

Abhay Shreeniwas Oka and Rajesh Bindal

Equivalent Citation: Criminal Appeal No. 1444 of 2023 (Arising out of SLP (Crl.) D. No. 28476 of 2018)

Case Reference:

Lakhvir Singh and Ors. v. The State of Punjab and Ors. MANU/SC/0026/2021

Tarak Nath Keshari vs. State of West Bengal (10.05.2023 - SC) : MANU/SC/0558/2023

NumberofPagesintheOriginalJudgment:4

Case Note:

Criminal -Probation - Benefit of - Section 7(1)(a)(ii) of Essential Commodities Act, 1955 and Section 4 of Probation of Offenders Act, 1958 - Appellant was tried and convicted under Section 7(1)(a)(ii) of Actfor violation ofWest Bengal Pulses, Edible Oil (Dealers Licensing) Order, 1978 - It was on account of fact that at time of inspection of his grocery shop, mustard oil and vegetable oil were found to be more than permissible limit - Trial Court sentenced Appellant to undergo rigorous imprisonment for a period of six months and imposed fine- In appeal, High Court upheld conviction, however, reduced sentence from rigorous imprisonment of six months to rigorous imprisonment of three monthshowever, fine was upheld - Hence, present appeal - Whether Appellant was entitled to benefit of probation.

Facts:

The Appellant was tried and convicted under Section 7(1)(a)(ii) of the Essential Commodities Act, 1955 for violation of para 3(1) of the West Bengal Pulses, Edible Oil (Dealers Licensing) Order, 1978. It was on account of the fact that at the time of inspection of his grocery shop, mustard oil and vegetable oil were found to be more than the permissible limit.The Trial Court sentenced the Appellant to undergo rigorous imprisonment for a period of six months and imposed a fine. The sale proceeds of the seized oil were forfeited to the State. In appeal, the High Court upheld the conviction, however, reduced the sentence from rigorous imprisonment of six months to rigorous imprisonment of three months. However, the fine was upheld.

Held, while disposing off the appeal:

i.   As far as the case of the Appellant on merits was concerned, this court did not find that any case was made out for interference in the concurrent findings of the facts recorded by all the courts below. It was found that the stock of mustard oil and vegetable oil found at the shop of the Appellant was more than the permissible limit, hence, this was violative of para 3(1) of the West Bengal Pulses, Edible Oil (Dealers Licensing) Order, 1978. [8]

ii. However, still this court found that a case was made out for grant of benefit of probation to the Appellant for the reason that the offence was committed more than thirty seven years back and it was not pointed out at the time of hearing that the Appellant was involved in any other offence. Before all the courts below, the Appellant remained on bail. While entertaining his appeal, even this Court had granted him exemption from surrendering. Section 4 of the Probation of Offenders Act, 1958 had a non obstante clause. [9]

Disposition: Disposed of

Mahalakshmi Sugar Mills Co. Ltd. and Ors. vs. Union of India (UOI) and Ors. (31.03.2008 - SC) : MANU/ SC/1772/2008

Relative Section:

Constitution Of India - Article 12, Article 14,Article 254(1); Essential Commodities Act, 1955 -Section 3,Section 3(2) (f), Section 3(3C),Section 3(3C)(a), Section 4, Section 5

Hon'bleJudges/Coram:

S.B. Sinha and V.S. Sirpurkar

Equivalent Citation: AIR2009SC792, 2009(3)ALT24(SC), JT2008(6)SC177, 2008(6)SCALE275, (2009)16SCC569, 2008(1)UJ611

Case Reference:

Bharat Petroleum Corporation Ltd. v. Maddula Ratnavalli and Ors. MANU/SC/7339/2007; Bombay Dyeing & Manufacturing Co. Ltd. v. Bombay Environmental Action Group MANU/SC/1197/2006; Commissioner of Income-Tax, West Bengal, Calcutta v. Gungadhar Banerjee & Co. (P) Ltd. MANU/SC/0161/1965; Delhi Farming & Construction (P) Ltd. v. Commissioner of Income Tax, Delhi MANU/SC/ 0246/2003; Godavari Sugar Mills Ltd. v. Union of India and Anr. JT 2001 (10) SC 527; In Re R.V. National Asylum Support Service (2002) 1 W.L.R.2956; Indian Express Newspapers (Bombay) Private Ltd. and Ors. v.

Union of India and Ors. ; Kuldip Chand and Anr. v. Advocate-General to Government of HP and Ors. (1990) 4 SCC 356; Life Insurance Corporation of India and Ors. v. Retired L.I.C. Officers Association and Ors. 2008 (2) SCALE 484; Malaprabha Co-op. Sugar Factory Ltd. v. Union of India and Anr. (Malaprabha-II) MANU/SC/1462/1997; Malaprabha Coop. Sugar Factory Ltd. v. Union of India and Anr. (Malaprabha-3) MANU/SC/2520/ 2000; Malaprabha Cooperative Sugar Factor v. Union of India (Malaprabha-I) since MANU/SC/0306/1994; Malaprabha Co-operative Sugar Factory Ltd. v. Union of India MANU/SC/0306/1994; Modi Industries Ltd. and Anr. v. Union of India and Ors. ; Modi Industries Ltd. v. Union of India and Anr. TC (C) No. 9 of 1990; New India Assurance Co. Ltd. v. Nusli Neville Wadia MANU/SC/0166/2008; Oriental Insurance Co. Ltd. v. Brij Mohan and Ors. MANU/SC/7682/2007; Pepper v. Hart (1993) A.C. 593; Shri Sitaram Sugar Company Ltd. and Anr. v. Union of India and Ors. MANU/SC/0249/1990; State of U.P. and Ors. v. Renusagar Power Co. and Ors. MANU/SC/0505/ 1988; The Panipat Co-operative Sugar Mills v. The Union of India MANU/ SC/0058/1972; The State of Karnataka and Anr. v. Shri Ranganatha Reddy and Anr. MANU/SC/0062/1977; Union of India and Ors. v. Triveni Engg. Works Ltd. and Ors. ; UP Sugar Mills Association and Ors. v. State of U.P. and Ors. 1997 (1) UPLBEC 541; Vasu Dev Singh v. Union of India MANU/ SC/8630/2006; Wilson v. First County Trust Ltd. [2004] 1 A.C. 816

NumberofPagesintheOriginalJudgment: 19

Case Note:

Commercial - Levy of sugar - Price determination - Requisite factors - Section 3(3C) of the Essential Commodities Act, 1955 - Clause 5A of the Sugarcane Control Order - U.P. Sugarcane (Regulation of Supply and Purchase) Act, 1953 - Appeals filed by various owners of sugar mills who purchased sugarcane from the farmers, concerns with the determination of price of sugar for the sugar years 1983-84 and 1984-85 - Central Government determined the price of levy sugar on the basis of 100 per cent mopping up - State of Uttar Pradesh under Section 16, U.P. Sugarcane (Regulation of Supply and Purchase) Act, 1953 enforced a price to be paid by the owners of the sugar mill to the producers known as State Advisory Price (ASP) - Writ applications were filed questioning the mode of calculation resorted to by the Central Government in determining the price of levy sugar, particularly, the effect of Clause 5A of the Sugarcane Control Order, as also ASP levied by the State - Divergent views were taken by Division Benches of the High Court - Hence, the present appeal

- Petitioners contended that 100 per cent mopping up was illegal and the liability of the sugar producers towards the cane growers was to be considered before arriving at the price of levy sugar - What are the factors which are required to be taken into consideration by the Central Government for determining the price of levy sugar in exercise of its power under Section 3(3C) of the Essential Commodities Act, 1955 - Held, direction by the Central Government to the owners of the sugar mills that a part of their products would be sold at a price determined by it is within its power under Section 3(2)(f) of the Act - Determination of price in terms of the provisions of the Act is a legislative function - However, if a price is determined without applying the principles underlying the factors enunciated in Section 3(3C) of the Act, the superior Courts can issue requisite direction - In the present case, the relevant factor that the Central Government has to take into consideration was Sub-Clause (iv) of Clause 5A of the Order which mandates that the additional price determination under Sub-Clause (ii) shall be paid by the producer of sugar to the sugarcane grower - If the actual price payable to the cane growers is absolutely relevant for determining the price of levy of sugar, then the effect of payment of an extra amount in terms of State Advisory Price cannot be refused to be taken into consideration - These elements would come either under Clause (b) or Clause (d) of Section 3(3C) of the Act - 100 per cent mopping held to be illegal - Direction to Central Government to re-fix the price of levy sugar while taking into consideration all the relevant factors - Appeal disposed of

Ratio Decidendi :

"If the actual price payable to the cane growers is absolutely relevant for determining the price of levy of sugar, then the effect of payment of an extra amount in terms of State Advisory Price cannot be refused to be taken into consideration while fixing the price of levy sugar."

Facts:

1. In these appeals, we are concerned with the determination of price of sugar for the sugar years 1983-84 and 1984-85.
2. What are the factors which are required to be taken into consideration by the Central Government for determining the price of levy sugar in exercise of its power under Section 3(3C) of the Essential Commodities Act, 1955 (the Act) is the question involved herein.
3. 3. Before us, there are various owners of sugar mills who purchased sugarcane from the farmers.

Section 3(2)(f) of the Act empowers the Central Government to fix compulsory quota of sugar produced by a sugar producer in the manner prescribed by the Central Government including the price thereof at which the same is to be sold. It is known as "levy sugar". The rest of the sugar, however, can be sold by the producers in free market. It is known as "free sugar".

1. The factors which are relevant to be taken into consideration by Central Government is contained in Section 3(3C) of the Act which includes:

(a) The minimum price, if any fixed for Sugarcane by the Central Government.

(b) The manufacturing cost of sugar.

(c) The duty or tax, if any, paid or payable thereon; and

(d) Securing a reasonable return on the Capital employed in the business of manufacturing, and different price may be determined from time to time for different areas or for different factories or for different kind of sugar.

Held by Hon'ble Court

1. Reliance placed by the learned Additional Solicitor General on Malaprabha-III is not apposite. This Court therein found the action of the Central Government to be not an act of contempt presumably because the directions were held to have been substantially complied with. We are not exercising any contempt jurisdiction. Contempt is a matter between the Court and the contemnor. We are herein called upon to determine as to which view of Delhi High Court in Hari Nagar or Mahalakshmi is correct. We cannot refuse to lay down the law having been called upon to do so. We must lay down a law for the future. We, therefore, while directing the Central Government to refix the price of levy sugar, would keep this direction confined only to the parties before us including the interveners. The reason therefore is that the other mill owners were not aggrieved thereby. The parties before us are fighting their grievance for more than 22 years. They should not be allowed to go empty handed.

2. We are, therefore, of the opinion that Mahalakshmi has wrongly been decided whereas Hari Nagar has correctly been decided.

3. Appeals arising out of SLP (C) Nos. 481/2007 and 14130/2007 filed by Mahalakshmi Sugar Mills Co. Ltd. and Govind Nagar Sugar Ltd. respectively are consequently allowed and Appeals arising out SLP (C) Nos. 14967-14978 of 2007 filed by Union of India and Ors. are dismissed. No

costs.

CHAPTER FIFTEEN

State of Maharashtra and Ors. vs. Lalit Somdatta Nagpal and Ors. (13.02.2007 - SC) : MANU / SC 7094 /2007

Relative Section:

Code of Civil Procedure, 1908 (CPC) - Section 82; Section 167(5); Section 262, Section 263, Section 264, Section 265, Section 438; Section 468; Essential Commodities (special Provisions) Act, 1981 [repealed] - Section 1(3), Section 7; Section 10, Essential Commodities Act, 1955 - Section 10A, Section 3, Section 7, Section 7(1)(a)(ii), Section 7A(1)(9)(ii), Section 9; General Clauses Act 1897 - Section 6; Indian Penal Code 1860, (IPC) - Section 120B; Section 302; Section 34; Section 364; Section 420; Section 468; Section 506(2); Maharashtra Control Of Organised Crime Act, 1999 - Section 1(ii), Section 2(1)(e), Section 2(a), Section 2(d), Section 2(d)(e), Section 2(e), Section 2(i)(d), Section 21, Section 21(3), Section 21(4), Section 23, Section 23(1), Section 23(1)(a), Section 3, Section 3(1)(2)(4), Section 7/

Hon'bleJudges/Coram:

A.R. Lakshmanan and Altamas Kabir

Equivalent Citation: Equivalent Citation: 2006 (Suppl.) ACC 837, I(2007)CCR435(SC), 2007CriLJ1678, JT2007(3)SC466, 2007(3)SCALE49, (2007)4SCC171, [2007]2SCR473, 2007(1)WLN118

NumberofPagesintheOriginalJudgment: 13

Case Reference:

Nirmal Kanti Roy v. State of West Bengal MANU/SC/0308/1998; West Bengal v. Falguni Dutta and Anr. MANU/SC/0530/1993; Ranjitsing Brahmjeetsing Sharma v. State of Maharashtra and Anr. MANU/SC/0268/2005; Durgesh Chandra Shah v. Vimal Chandra Shah MANU/SC/0200/1996

Case Note:

Constitution - Applicability - Sections 3, 7 and 11 of Essential Commodities (Special Provisions) Act, 1981, Sections 3 and 7 of Essential Commodities Act, 1955 and Sections 2(a) and 23 of Maharashtra Control of Organized Crime Act, 1999 Special leave petitions raising common question of law relating to application of provisions of Act of 1999 in respect of offences committed under Sections 3 and 7 having particular regard to enactment of Act of 1981 High Court held that since trials under Act of 1955 to be tried by Special Court in summary way for which maximum sentence of two years can be imposed provisions of MCOCA had no application - Held, limitation of power to impose punishment only for maximum period of two years for offence under 1981 Act did not preclude authorities from applying provisions of MCOCA for offences under Sections 3 & 7 of 1955 Act as well as 1981 Act

Ratio Decidendi:

"Applicability-MCOCA,1999 vis a vis offence under Essential Commodities Act, 1955 -Limitation of power to impose punishment only for maximum period of two years for offence under 1981 Act did not preclude authorities from applying provisions of MCOCA for offences under Sections 3 & 7 of 1955 Act as well as 1981 Act "

Case Category:

CRIMINAL MATTERS - MATTERS RELATING TO BANK SCAMS, CHEATING, FORGERY ETC.

Facts:

1. Five Special Leave Petitions, of which three have been filed by the State of Maharashtra, one by Lalit Somdatta Nagpal and one by Kapil Nagpal, have been taken up for hearing together as they involve common questions of law relating to the application of the provisions of the Maharashtra Control of Organized Crime Act, 1999 in respect of offences alleged to have been committed under Sections 3 and 7 of the Essential Commodities Act, 1955. In order to answer the above question, it is

necessary to briefly set out the facts involved in these Special Leave
Petitions.

2. On 6th June, 2004 the Deputy Commissioner of Police (Enforcement),
Crime Branch, Mumbai alongwith other officers, including the District
Supply Officer, Kolhapur, Nayab Tehsildar, Taluka Karveer, Distt. Kolhapur,
raided Vijayanand Petrol Pump, Kolhapur and seized two iron tanks of
12,000 and 6,000 litres capacity, greenish lubricating oil in 200 litres barrel,
45 kilos of white chemical powder in 5 gunny bags and ten motor tankers
containing petroleum products and two empty tankers, worth Rs.
77,14,195/-, and arrested 9 persons in connection therewith. On the
statement made by Ranjit Pandurang Desai, Nayab Tehsildar, Karveer
Taluka, a case was registered at Karveer Police Station, Kolhapur, being C.R.
No. 39/2004, under Sections 3 and 7 of the Essential Commodities Act,
1955 and under Section 3 of the Petroleum Storage and Distribution Act,
2000 against 11 accused persons. Out of the 11 accused persons 10 were
arrested and produced before the Chief Judicial Magistrate, Kolhapur, and
remanded to judicial custody on 7th May, 2004. On 20th May 2004, on the
orders of the Director General of Police, the investigation into the alleged
offence was transferred to CB (Control), Crime Branch, Worli, Mumbai.

3. On an application made by the prosecution for police custody of the
accused persons, the Fast Track Court, Kolhapur, by its order dated 25th
May, 2004 remanded the accused persons to police custody from judicial
custody. On 27th May, 2004, Lalit Nagpal, Ranjana Nagpal, Anil Nagpal, Vijay
Nagpal and Chetan Mehta moved the Sessions Judge, Kolhapur, for grant of
anticipatory bail and although initially protection was given from arrest, on
14th June, 2004 the Sessions Judge rejected the anticipatory bail applications
of all the applicants except that of Ranjana Nagpal, the wife of the accused
Lalit Nagpal. The second anticipatory bail application filed by Anil Nagpal,
Chetan Mehta and Lalit Nagpal by way of three separate Writ Petitions were
rejected by the High Court. The Writ Petition filed by Vijay Nagpal was
allowed while the others were directed to surrender before the Police on or
before 20th August 2004.

4. The said Anil Nagpal, Lalit Nagpal and Chetan Mehta thus filed Special
Leave Petitions against the order of the Bombay High Court and renewed
their prayer for anticipatory bail before this Court. This Court also initially
directed that the applicants be not arrested and directed them to attend
the Police Station every day. Subsequently, however, on 14th December,
2004 the Special Leave Petitions were dismissed and the petitioners therein

were directed to surrender and apply for regular bail before the Trial Court. Thereafter, on 19th January, 2005, Lalit Somdatta Nagpal filed Criminal Writ Petition No. 44 of 2005 in the High Court challenging the approval order dated 31stOctober 2004 passed under Section 23(1)(a) of the Maharashtra Control of Organized Crime Act, 1999 (hereinafter referred to as "MCOCA")

5. Accused Chetan Mehta also filed a writ petition, being No. 276 of 2004, in the Bombay High Court also challenging the approval order dated 31stOctober, 2004 under Section 23(1)(a) of the above Act. The said two writ petitions were heard by the High Court along with Writ Petition No. 2562 of 2004 filed by the accused, Deepak Dwarkadas Mundado, on 2ndFebruary, 2005. On the said date the writ petition of Deepak Mundada was permitted to be withdrawn and the remaining two writ petitions were adjourned till 10th February, 2005 and again till 17th February, 2005, when one of the other accused, Anil Nagpal, filed Writ Petition No. 146 of 2005. By judgment dated 11th March, 2005, Bombay High Court allowed the writ petitions filed by Lalit Nagpal and Anil Nagpal upon holding that having regard to the provisions of the Essential Commodities Act, 1955 and the Essential Commodities (Special Provisions) Act, 1981, the provisions of MCOCA would have no application to the cases against the petitioners. The State of Maharashtra has filed S.L.P.(Crl.) Nos. 3320-21 of 2005 against the said judgment of the Bombay High Court.

6. Though, for reasons which are different from those given while allowing the writ petitions filed by Lalit Nagpal and Anil Nagpal, the Bombay Court in a separate judgment issued rule and granted interim relief in Criminal Writ Petition No. 2183 of 2005 filed by Lalit Nagpal & Ors. seeking to quash CR II-B of 2005 registered with Rasayani P.S., Raigad, and also for quashing the investigation proceedings under MCOCA. The State has filed SLP(Crl) No. 1101 of 2006 against the interim order passed by the Bombay High Court in Criminal Writ Petition No. 2183 of 2005.

7. Special Leave Petition (Criminal) 4581 of 2006 has been filed by Lalit Nagpal against the order of the Bombay High Court dated 14th July, 2006 whereby Lalit Nagpal's prayer for bail in Crl. Application No. 1057 of 2006 was rejected, but the second application, being Crl. Application No. 348 of 2006, for shifting the applicant to a particular hospital, was directed to be placed before the appropriate Court taking up such applications. The fifth and last Special Leave Petition (Crl.) No. 4611 of 2006 has been filed by Kapil Lalit Nagpal against the order dated 1stSeptember 2006 passed by

the Bombay High Court in his Criminal Writ Petition No. 2183 of 2005 directing him to surrender before the Reviewing Authority at Kolhapur within two weeks, failing which his petition, inter alia, for restraining the respondents from arresting him and stay of further investigation in Rasayani P.S., Raigad, C.R. No. II-B/2005, would stand dismissed.

As the common question of law in all these Special Leave Petitions relate to the applicability of MCOCA to the offences alleged to have been committed by Lalit Nagpal and Kapil Nagpal, we have heard the matters together and are disposing of all the five petitions by this common judgment.

Held by Hon'ble Court

1. In our view, both the sanctions which formed the very basis of the investigation have been given mechanically and are vitiated and cannot be sustained. In taking recourse to the provisions of the MCOCA 1999, which has the effect of curtailing the liberty of an individual and keeping him virtually incarcerated, a great responsibility has been cast on the authorities in ensuring that the provisions of the Act are strictly adhered to and followed, which unfortunately does not appear to have been done in the instant case.[44]

2. We are not, therefore, inclined to interfere with the decision of the High Court though for reasons which are entirely different from those given by the High Court. The Special Leave Petitions (Crl.) Nos. 3320-3321/2005 filed by the State of Maharashtra are, therefore, dismissed. For the same reasons, Special Leave Petition (Crl.) No. 1101/2006 filed by the State of Maharashtra must also fail and the High Court will now have to dispose of the application filed by the petitioners in Crl.Writ Petition No. 2183/2005 for quashing C.R. No. II-8/2005 registered with Rasayani Police Station, Raigad.[45]

3. As far as Special Leave Petition (Crl.) No. 4581/2006 is concerned, the same has been filed against the order passed by the Bombay High Court rejecting the petitioner's prayer for grant of bail. As will be seen from the records, the petitioner had earlier applied for grant of anticipatory bail which was rejected by the Bombay High Court. In the Special Leave Petition filed against the said order of rejection, this Court also on 14th December, 2004 rejected the petitioner's prayer for grant of anticipatory bail. This Court however granted 15 days' time to the petitioner to surrender and to apply for regular bail. Despite the said order, the petitioner did not surrender till 1stJuly 2005, and thereafter applied for bail which was

rejected on the ground that the petitioner had violated the order passed by this Court on 14th December, 2004 and had absconded for almost six months before surrendering. The order passed by this Bombay High Court rejecting the petitioner's prayer for bail was again challenged before this Court and the same was once again dismissed on 20th January, 2006 with the observation that such dismissal would not bar the petitioner to approach the trial court afresh. Thereafter, the petitioner moved a fresh application for bail before the Sessions Court which was rejected on 3rdMarch, 2006. The petitioner challenged the order of the Sessions Court in the Bombay High Court which once again dismissed the petitioner's prayer for grant of bail on the ground that the circumstances had not changed except that the prayer for enlarging the petitioner on had been made bail on medical grounds. While rejecting the petitioner's prayer for bail, the High Court observed that on the basis of the medical report, no case had been made out for enlarging the petitioner on bail. However, the prayer as regards shifting the applicant to a particular hospital would have to be considered on its own merits.[46]

Special Leave Petition (Crl.) No. 4581/2006 is directed against the said order of the High Court refusing to grant bail to the petitioner.

4. It may be indicated that during the pendency of the writ petition, this Court on a consideration of the medical condition of the petitioner permitted him to be treated in a private hospital, though under the custody of the respondents. We understand that the petitioner continues to be hospitalized. Having regard to the fact that we have dismissed the Special Leave Petitions filed by the State of Maharashtra against the order of the Bombay High Court holding that the provisions of MCOCA had been misapplied to the facts of the case, the stringent provisions regarding bail under the MCOCA 1999 will no longer be attracted in this case. Since the petitioner has been under arrest since the date of his surrender on 1stJuly, 2005, and having further regard to his medical condition, we direct that the petitioner, Lalit Somdutt Nagpal, be released on bail to the satisfaction of the Chief Judicial Magistrate, Kolhapur. He will surrender his passport to the Chief Judicial Magistrate, Kolhapur, until further orders of the magistrate and will not leave the country without the prior permission of the magistrate and shall report to the Investigating Officer of the different cases as and when called upon to do so. Special Leave Petition (Crl.) No. 4581/2006 is accordingly allowed and the order of the Bombay High Court dated 14th July, 2006 refusing the petitioner's prayer for grant of bail is set

aside.[47]

5. As far as Special Leave Petition (Crl.) No. 4611/2006 is concerned, since we have held hereinbefore while deciding the Special Leave Petitions filed by the State of Maharashtra that Kapil Lalit Nagpal had been wrongly proceeded against under the provisions of the MCOCA 1999, we allow the special leave petition and set aside the order passed by the Bombay High Court on 1stSeptember, 2006 in Crl. Writ Petition No. 2183/2005 with a direction to hear out the petitioner's said writ petition in accordance with law.[48]

There will be no order as to costs in any of these special leave petitions.[49]

CHAPTER SIXTEEN

The State of Uttar Pradesh vs. Aman Mittal and Ors. (04.09.2019 - SC) : MANU/SC/1202/2019

Relative Section:

Code of Criminal Procedure, 1973 (CrPC) - Section 153, Section 167(2), Section 173(8), Section 190, Section 190(1), Section 482; Essential Commodities Act, 1955 - Section 3, Section 7; Food Safety and Standards Act, 2006 - Section 55; General Clauses Act, 1897 - Section 26; Indian Penal Code, 1860 (IPC) - Section 34, Section 114, Section 120B,Section 188, Section 264,Section 265, Section 266, Section 267, Section 272, Section 273,Section 292, - Section 294, Section 328,Section 406, Section 415, Section 420, Section 467, Section 468, Section 471; Information Technology Act, 2000 - Section 43, Section 43(a), Section 43(j),Section 66, - Section 67, Section 67A,Section 67B,Section 79, Section 81; Karnataka Civil Services (General Recruitment) Rules, 1977 - Rule 1(3);Rule 3, Rule 3(1),Rule 3(2),Rule 4, Rule 4(2); Karnataka General Service (Motor Vehicles Branch) (Recruitment) Rules, 1976; Legal Metrology Act, 2009 - Section 3, Section 12, Section 26, Section 30,Section 51; Negotiable Instruments Act, 1881 - Section 138; Standards of Weights and Measures Act, 1976 - Section 12,Section 30

Hon'bleJudges/Coram:

L. Nageswara Rao and Hemant Gupta

Equivalent Citation: 2020(1)ACR779, 2019(202)AIC37, 2019 (109) ACC 176, 2019(3) Crimes376 (SC) , 2019/INSC/1001, 2019(4)J.L.J.R.218,

2019 (4) KHC 696, 2020(1)KLT260, 2020(1)N.C.C.716, 2019 (4) PLJR 244 , 2019(4)RCR(Criminal)253, 2019(12)SCALE41, (2019)19SCC740, [2019]11SCR1180

NumberofPagesintheOriginalJudgment:18

Case Reference:

M.C. Abraham and Anr. v. State of Maharashtra and Ors. MANU/SC/1190/2002;

State of Bihar and Anr. v. J.A.C. Saldanha and Ors. MANU/SC/0253/1979;

Sangeetaben Mahendrabhai Patel v. State of Gujarat and Anr. MANU/SC/0321/2012;

Sharat Babu Digumarti v. Govt. of NCT of Delhi MANU/SC/1592/2016;

Shreya Singhal v. Union of India (UOI) MANU/SC/0329/2015;

Khoday Distilleries Ltd. and Ors. v. Sri Mahadeshwara Sahakara Sakkare Karkhane Ltd. MANU/SC/0306/2019;

Workmen of Cochin Port Trust v. Board of Trustees of The Cochin Port Trust and Anr. MANU/SC/0291/1978; Management of Western India Match Company, Ltd. v. Industrial Tribunal and Anr. MANU/TN/0017/1958; Indian Oil Corporation Ltd. v. State of Bihar and others MANU/SC/0572/1986;

Rup Diamonds and Ors. v. Union of India and Ors. MANU/SC/0358/1989;

Supreme Court Employees' Welfare Association and Ors. v. Union of India (UOI) and Anr. MANU/SC/0582/1989;

Yogendra Naryana Chowdhury and other v. Union of India and other MANU/SC/0203/1996;

V.M. Salgaocar & Bros. Pvt. Ltd. v. Commissioner of Income Tax MANU/SC/0271/2000;

Sree Narayana Dharmasanghom Trust v. Swami Prakasananda and Ors. MANU/SC/1267/1997;

State of Maharashtra and another v. Prabhakar Bhikaji Ingle MANU/SC/0804/1996;

Penu Balakrishna Iyer and Ors. v. Ariya M. Ramaswami Iyer and Ors. MANU/SC/0238/1964;

Abbai Maligai Partnership Firm and Anr. v. K. Santhakumaran and Ors. MANU/SC/1141/1998;

Shankar Ramchandra Abhyankar v. Krishnaji Dattatreya Bapat MANU/SC/0456/1969;

Sushil Kumar Scn v. State of Bihar MANU/SC/0028/1975;

Gopabandhu Biswal v. Krishna Chandra Mohanty and Ors. MANU/SC/1015/1998;

Junior Telecom Officers Forum and others v. Union of India and others MANU/SC/0108/1993;

Thungabhadra Industries Ltd. v. The Government of Andhra Pradesh MANU/SC/0217/1963;

Kunhayammed & Ors. v. State of Kerala & Anr. MANU/SC/0432/2000;

T.S. Baliah v. T.S. Rengachari MANU/SC/0238/1968;

State of Bihar v. Murad Ali Khan and Ors. MANU/SC/0470/1988;

Macquarie Bank Limited v. Shilpi Cable Technologies Ltd. MANU/SC/1609/2017;

Commercial Tax Officer, Rajasthan v. Binani Cements Ltd. and Anr. MANU/SC/0121/2014;

R.S. Raghunath v. State of Karnataka and another MANU/SC/0012/1992;

State of Maharashtra v. Sayyed Hassan Criminal Appeal No. 1195 of 2018;

Gagan Harsh Sharma and Anr. v. The State of Maharashtra and Anr. Criminal Writ Petition No. 4361 of 2018 ;

Wilson v. Colchester Justices MANU/UKHL/0028/1985 : (1985) 2 All ER 97 (HL);

Edmond v. United States MANU/USSC/0045/1997: 137 L Ed 2d 917: 520 US 651 (1997);

Warden v. Marrero MANU/USSC/0099/1974: 41 L Ed 2d 383: 417 US 653 (1974)

Case Note:

Criminal - Applicability of Act - Sections 34,120B,265,267,467,468 and 471 of Indian Penal Code, 1860, Sections 3 and 7 of Essential Commodities Act, 1955 and Sections 12 and 30 of Legal Metrology Act, 2009 - FIR was lodged against accused persons for offences punishable under Sections 265, 267, 420, 34, 120-B of Code and Sections 3 and 7 of Act, 1955 in respect of short delivery of petrol and diesel - Charge-sheet for offences under Sections 265, 267, 420, 34, 120B of Code and Sections 3 and 7 of Act 1955, Sections 467, 468, 471 of Code and Sections 12 and 30 of Act, 1976 came to be filed before competent court - Magistrate did not take cognizance of offence under Sections 471 and 120B of Code for want of evidence but Magistrate had taken cognizance of offence under Section 30 of Act - On petition before High Court for quashing of charge sheet, High Court held that procedure of investigation, inquiry and trial under Code of Criminal Procedure would accordingly apply inasmuch as, no procedure in relation thereto was prescribed under Special Act - It was further held that Section 26 of Act overrides provisions of Indian Penal Code as Section 51 of Act clearly excludes application of Indian Penal Code and Section 153 of Code - Hence, present appeal - Whether procedure of investigation, inquiry and trial under Code of Criminal Procedure would apply to Legal Metrology Act, 2009.

Facts:

An FIR was lodged for the offences punishable under Sections 265, 267, 420, 34, 120-B of the Indian Penal Code, 1860 and Sections 3 and 7 of the Essential Commodities Act, 19552 in respect of short delivery of petrol and diesel. The charge-sheet for the offences under Sections 265, 267, 420, 34, 120B Indian Penal Code and Sections 3 and 7 of the Act, 1955, Sections 467, 468, 471 Indian Penal Code and Sections 12 and 30 of the Weights and Measures Act, 1976 came to be filed before the competent court. The Magistrate did not take cognizance of offence under Sections 471 and 120B of Indian Penal Code for want of evidence but the Magistrate had taken cognizance of an offence under Section 30 of the Act. It was thereafter applications were filed under Sections 167(2) and 190(1) of the Code of Criminal Procedure, 1973 on the ground that the prosecution had no material making out a case of offences mentioned in the chargesheet, therefore, the cognizance may not be taken. The Magistrate rejected both the applications. On petition, the High Court held that the procedure of investigation, inquiry and trial under the Code of Criminal Procedure would accordingly apply inasmuch as, no procedure in relation thereto is prescribed under the Special Act. It was further held that Section 26 of the Act overrides the provisions of Sections 264 to 267 of Indian Penal Code as Section 51 of the Act clearly excludes the application of Indian Penal Code and Section 153 of the Code insofar as it relates with regard to weights and measures punishable under the special Act.

Held, while partly allowing the appeal:

(i) There was no merit in the argument of Appellant that the Legal Metrology Act, 2009 was a complete Code which contains the provisions of offences and penalties under the said Act, therefore, for any violation of the provisions of the Act, the prosecution could be lodged only under the Act and not for the offences even if disclosed under Indian Penal Code. [18]

(ii) Section 51 of the Legal Mctrology Act, 2009 provides that the provisions of Indian Penal Code and of Section 153 of the Code insofar as such provisions relate to offences with regard to weight and measures only shall not apply to any offence which was punishable under the Act. Section 153 of the Code permits an officer in charge of police station to enter any place for the purpose of inspecting or searching any weights or measures or instruments for weighing, used or kept therein. Section 153 of the Code had been made inapplicable under the Act as power of search and seizure was vested with the designated authorities under the Act. Therefore, the entire Code was inapplicable in respect of the prosecution under the Act that the police could not enter any place for the purpose of inspecting or searching for any weights or measures. [31]

(iii) Section 3 of the Act completely overrides the provisions of Chapter XIII of Indian Penal Code in respect of the offences and penalties imposable for violations of the provisions of the Act, it being special Act. Therefore, if the offence was disclosed to be made out under the provisions of the Act, an Accused could not be charged for the same offence under Chapter XIII of Indian Penal Code. Reading of Section 51 of the Act makes it clear that the provisions of Indian Penal Code insofar as they relate to offences with regard to weight or measure, shall not apply to any offence which was punishable under the Act. Therefore, the provisions of Indian Penal Code which relate to offences with regard to weight and measure as contained in Chapter XIII of Indian Penal Code alone will not apply. No person could be charged for an offence relating to weight or measure falling under Chapter XIII of Indian Penal Code in view of the provisions of the Act. [34]

(iv) The scheme of the Act is for the offences for use of weights and measures which are non-standard and for tampering with or altering any standards, secondary standards or working standards of any weight or measure. The Act did not foresee any offence relating to cheating as defined in Section 415 of Indian Penal Code or the offences under Sections 467, 468 and 471 of Indian Penal Code. Similarly, an act performed in furtherance of a common intention disclosing an offence under Section 34 was not covered by the provisions of the Act. An offence disclosing a criminal conspiracy to commit an offence which was punishable under Section 120-B Indian Penal Code was also not an offence under the Act. Since such offences were not punishable under the provisions of the Act, therefore, the prosecution for such offences could be maintained since the trial of such offences was not inconsistent with any of the provisions of the Act. Similar was the provision in respect of the offences under Sections 467, 468, 471 Indian Penal Code as such offences were not covered by the provisions of the Act. [35]

(v) Therefore, upheld the order of the High Court that the offences under Sections 265 and 267 Indian Penal Code were liable to be quashed. The directions of the High Court in proceedings under Section 482 of the Code against the interest of the Accused in a petition filed by the Accused were beyond the jurisdiction of the High Court and, thus, all such observations and directions were quashed. The directions issued by the High Court that the erring officers/officials named in the supplementary report shall be subject to disciplinary action were again beyond the scope of the High Court in a petition under Section 482 of the Code seeking quashing of the charge-sheet and were, thus, quashed. [36]

Disposition: Appeal Partly Allowed RPG Life Sciences Ltd. and Ors. vs. State of Tamil Nadu(11.05.2010-SC):MANU/SC/0370/2010

Relative Section:

Essential Commodities Act, 1955 - Section 3(2)(c), Section 7(1)(a)(ii)

Hon'bleJudges/Coram:

Dalveer Bhandari and Aftab Alam

Equivalent Citation: Equivalent Citation: 2010(2)ACR1882(SC), 2010(90)AIC12, AIR2010SC2765, 2010 (71) ACC 285, 2010 (80) ALR 936, 2010(4)BLJ40, III(2010)CCR37(SC), 2010(3)Crimes27(SC), 2010(3)RCR(Civil)210, 2010(3)RCR(Criminal)366, 2010(5)SCALE582, (2010)6SCC540

NumberofPagesintheOriginalJudgment:5

Case Reference: nil

Case Note:

Essential Commodities Act, 1955 - Section 7 (1) (a) (ii) read with Section 3 (2) (c)-Drugs (Prices Control) Order, 1979 (D.P.C.O.)-Para 20-Violation of para 20 of D.P.C.O. for not indicating M.R.P. on drugs-Conviction and sentence-Whether invites any interference?-Held, "partly"-

Instead of sending appellants to jail after 25 years-Sentence of fine substantially increased.

The accused appellants were convicted under para 20 of D.P.C.O. 1979 and were punished by the Special Judge under the Essential Commodities Act, 1955 sentencing them to three months' imprisonment and fine.

In the present case, the incident is of 31.5.1985 and in the peculiar facts of this case it may not be desirable to send the appellants to jail after a lapse of about 25 years.[Para 17] In the facts and circumstances of this case, ends of justice would meet if while maintaining the conviction of the appellants, instead of sending them to serve out three months of imprisonment, the sentence of fine is substantially increased.

Case Category:

CRIMINAL MATTERS - MATTERS RELATING TO ESSENTIAL COMMODITIES ACT

Industry: Pharmaceutical

Facts:

Brief facts which are necessary to dispose of these appeals are recapitulated as under:

1.On 29.11.1985, the then Drugs Inspector, Park Town, II Range, Office of the Assistant State Drugs Controller Zone-1, inspected the premises of M/s. Sri Mahaveer Pharma Agencies (appellant No. 1 in Crl. A. No. 1034 of 2002) and found 68 bottles containing 100 Tablets each of Haloperidol, 5 Mg. Tablets, B.P. Lot 060, which was manufactured in March 1985 by M/s. Searle India Limited (now M/s. RPG Life Sciences Ltd.). He also found that the bottles do not contain the labels indicating the maximum retail price of the Drug as contemplated under the Drugs (Prices Control) Order, 1979 (hereinafter referred to as 'DPCO 1979'). The said bottles were frozen on 29.11.1985 and at the same time, he also found that there were no purchase details for the purchase of the said bottles. Acknowledging the same, Padamchand Chordia, partner of the firm M/s. Sri Mahaveer Pharma Agencies, submitted a letter (Ex.P1) stating that the labels do not indicate the maximum retail price and they agreed to furnish the purchase and sale details of Haloperidol 5 Mg. Tablets. On 2.12.1985, the Drugs Inspector drew samples from the bottles under Form No. 17, marked as Ex.P.-3 and attested by P.W.3. Based on the above, show cause notices were sent to the respective firms and on the replies from the accused and the reports from the analyst, a complaint was filed by the Drugs Inspector against seven accused persons.

2. First accused is M/s. Searle India Limited, Bombay which is the manufacturing firm of the Drug Heloperidol Tablet;

Second accused is Dr. K.K. Maheshwari, Production Manager of M/s. Searle India Limited, Bombay;

Third accused is the firm by name M/s. Sri Mahaveer Pharma Agencies, who had purchased, sold and stocked the drug Haloperidol Tablets manufactured by A-1 Company;

Fourth accused is the partner by name Padamchand Chordia representing the accused firm M/s. Sri Mahaveer Pharma Agencies;

Fifth accused is the firm by name M/s. Sri Mahaveer Pharma Distributors who purchased, sold and stocked Haloperidol Tablet;

Sixth accused is the partner by name Padamchand Chordia of M/s. Mahaveer Pharma Distributors (A-5) who purchased, sold and stocked the drug Haloperidol; and

Seventh accused by name, Raghavan, is the Proprietor of the firm M/s. Sripathy Distributors Madras, who purchased and sold Haloperidol Tablet.

3. The above seven accused were charged for violation of para 20 of the DPCO 1979 punishable under Section 7(1)(a)(ii) of the Essential Commodities Act, 1955 read with Section 3(2)(c) of the said Act. The Special Judge, Essential Commodities Act, Madras tried the charges and found the accused appellants guilty of the charges and convicted all of them under Section 7(1)(a)(ii) of the Essential Commodities Act, 1955 read with Section 3(2)(c) of the said Act and sentenced them as follows:

Held by Hon'ble Court

1. In the present case, the incident is of 31.5.1985 and in the peculiar facts of this case it may not be desirable to send the appellants to jail after a lapse of about 25 years.

2. In the facts and circumstances of this case, we are of the considered view that ends of justice would meet if while maintaining the conviction of the appellants, instead of sending them to serve out three months of imprisonment, the sentence of fine is substantially increased.

3. We, therefore, direct Appellant No. 1 Company to pay a fine Rs. 2 lakhs, instead of Rs. 10,000/-, as directed by the Trial Court and confirmed by the High court. Other appellants i.e accused Nos. 2 to 6 are directed to pay a fine Rs. 25,000/- each. We extend this order to one Mr. Raghavan (accused No. 7) who has not filed an appeal before this Court. The accused are directed to pay the said amount of fine within a period of six weeks from today. In case the aforesaid amount of fine is not paid within six weeks, this

order would not be of any avail to the accused and they will have to serve out the sentences as directed by the Trial Court and confirmed by the High Court.

4. With this modification of the Trial Court order as affirmed by the High Court, these appeals are disposed of in the aforementioned terms.

CHAPTER EIGHTEEN

Oudh Sugar Mills Ltd. vs. Union of India (UOI) and Ors. (07.02.2020 - SC) : MANU/SC/0153/2020

Relative Section:

Constitution of India - Article 14, Article 19(1), Article 226; Essential Commodities Act, 1955 - Section 3(2), Section 3(3c); Sugar (Price Determination for 1984-85 production) Order, 1984; Sugar (Price Determination for 1985-86 Production) Order, 1985

Hon'bleJudges/Coram:

Mohan M. Shantanagoudar and R. Subhash Reddy, JJ.

Equivalent Citation: Equivalent Citation: 2020(214)AIC257, AIR2020SC1773, 2020 (143) ALR 218, 2020 6 AWC5223SC, 2020 (4) CCC 426 , 2020/INSC/143, 2020(6)MhLj46, (2020)4SCC29, [2020]2SCR619

NumberofPagesintheOriginalJudgment: 5

Case Reference: nil

Case Note:

Civil - Placing of unit - Denial of permission - Appellant filed writ before High Court directing opposite parties to place Petitioners' sugar factory in East U.P. Zone for purposes of Sugar Order, 1984 and Sugar Order, 1985 - It was case of Appellant that Appellant factory was discriminated against and kept in central zone for purpose of fixation of levy sugar price - High Court dismissed writ petition by holding that said decision was policy decision which permitted Central Government to make reasonable classification - Hence, present appeal - Whether Appellant's unit was directed to be placed in eastern zone instead of central zone.

Facts:

The Appellant company filed writ petition before the High Court for directing the opposite parties to place the Petitioners' sugar factory in East U.P. Zone for the purposes of the Sugar Order, 1984 and Sugar Order, 1985 and also directing the opposite parties to permit the Petitioner company to realise the price of their levy sugar as admissible to the sugar factories in the East U.P. Zone under the Sugar Order, 1984 and Sugar Order, 1985. It was the case of the Appellant that the Appellant factory was discriminated against and kept in the central zone for the purpose of fixation of levy sugar price. Considering the submissions made on behalf of both the sides and other material placed on record, the High Court, by recording a finding that the said decision was a policy decision which permitted the Central Government to make a reasonable classification and in absence of any case made out either of arbitrariness or hostile discrimination, dismissed the writ petition filed by the Appellant.

Held, while dismissing the appeal:

(i) The price of levy sugar was fixed for a zone with an intention to ensure to the manufacturers of the sugar in the zone a reasonable return on their overall production and investment, provided that the units are running economically and efficiently. Sugar was a controlled commodity during the relevant time, covered by the provisions of the Essential Commodities Act, 1955. Certain quantity of sugar called levy sugar, was to be supplied to the Government at a price fixed by the Government and rest of the same was levy free sugar, which could be sold in open market. The price of levy sugar was fixed based on the Control Order framed under the Essential Commodities Act. The price of levy sugar was fixed by the Central Government, having regard to various factors, including the basis of basic-cost schedules drawn and recommended by the expert body. As was evident from the stand of the Respondents it appears that the survey report of Bureau of Industrial Cost and Prices (BICP) regarding the zonal pattern was not found feasible by the Government of India and the same was not implemented. The Appellant had claimed parity with sugar factories at Biswan and Mahmoodabad, but such units were transferred to eastern zone on merits adjudged by the State Government and BICP and levy prices were fixed for zones and not for each factory. Zones were also not as per the revenue districts. Merely because there was difference in price in central zone and eastern zone, the Appellant could not claim, as a matter of right, its unit was to be placed in eastern zone instead of central zone during the relevant years. The impugned Orders questioned in the writ petition were based on exhaustive study by experts. The conclusions reached by the Central Government in exercise of statutory power could not be said to be either discriminatory or unreasonable. So far as sugar units at Biswan and Mahmoodabad were concerned, they were transferred to eastern zone on the basis of merits adjudged by the State. When the revenue districts were not the limits for zonal division, the Appellant could not claim parity with other units only on the ground that all the units are situated in Sitapur district. Even with regard to Appellant unit, after a lapse of time it was considered feasible to place it in eastern zone and we are informed that the same was placed in eastern zone. As the Appellant has failed to demonstrate any invidious discrimination and statutory violation, merely on the ground that other units in Sitapur district were transferred to eastern zone and that the representation of the Appellant was not acceded to for the relevant crushing years, was no ground for interference. This court was not persuaded to accept the plea that the Appellant was discriminated against by placing the Appellant unit in central zone and other units in Sitapur district in the eastern zone of Uttar Pradesh. The action of the Central Government in placing the factory of the Appellant at two different times in two different zones also does not constitute any discrimination. The policy decision was taken from time to time subject to satisfaction of the Government by taking into account expert reports. It was also the case of the Respondents that the factory at Mahmoodabad was established at a very higher free sale sugar over the normal quota as per incentive scheme of Government. Several relevant factors were considered by the State Government before announcing policy and for fixation of zones. Therefore, there was no illegality in the impugned order dismissing the Writ Petition. [7]

Disposition: Appeal Dismissed
Industry: Sugar

CHAPTER NINETEEN

Santosh vs. The State of Maharashtra (10.10.2017 - SC) : MANU/SC/1313/2017

Relative Section:

Essential Commodities Act, 1955 - Section 3, Section 7; Indian Penal Code, 1860 (IPC) - Section 408; Code of Criminal Procedure, 1973 (CrPC) - Section 161; Constitution of India - Article 20(3)

Hon'bleJudges/Coram:

Kurian Joseph and R. Banumath

Equivalent Citation: 2017(3)ACR3231, 2018(184)AIC150, 2018 (103) ACC 302, 2017ALLMR(Cri) 4882 , 2017(4)BLJ200, IV(2017)CCR164(SC), 2018(1)ECrN 4, (2018)2GLR914, 2017/INSC/1027, 2018(1)N.C.C.159, 2017(4)RCR(Criminal)590, 2017(12)SCALE524, (2017)9SCC714, 2017 (10) SCJ 531, [2017]10SCR129, 2017(3)UC2126

NumberofPagesintheOriginalJudgment: 4

Case Reference:

Selvi and Ors. v. State of Karnataka MANU/SC/0325/2010 :

Case Note:

Criminal - Anticipatory bail - Entitlement thereto - Section 408 of Indian Penal Code, 1860 and Sections 3 and 7 of Essential Commodities Act, 1955 - Appellant was one of Accused in crime registered for offences under Section 408 of Code read with Sections 3 and 7 of Act - Additional Sessions Judge, rejected application for anticipatory bail - High Court as per order was also of same view, although same Court had initially granted interim protection - Hence, present appeal - Whether Appellant was entitled for anticipatory bail.

Facts:

The Appellant was one of the Accused in crime registered for offences under Section 408 of Code read with Sections 3 and 7 of Act. The allegation was that he received misappropriated food-grains meant for public distribution. In the order Additional Sessions Judge, rejected the application for anticipatory bail. The High Court as per order was also of the same view, although the same Court had initially granted interim protection. Thus aggrieved, Hence, present appeal.

Held, while disposing off the appeal:

(i) The Investigating Officer (IO) was of the view that the custody of the Appellant was required for recording his confessional statement in terms of what the co-accused had already stated. The IO was of the opinion that the Appellant was not cooperating because he kept reiterating that he had not purchased the food-grains. The purpose of custodial interrogation was not just for the purpose of confession. In case there was no cooperation on the part of the Appellant for the completion of the investigation, it would be open to the Respondent to approach the Sessions Court, in which case the Sessions Court having regard to the materials already collected by the Investigating Officer, if so satisfied that the custodial interrogation of the Appellant was still required for completion of the investigation, would be free to pass appropriate orders. [7] and[9]

Disposition: Disposed of

Malaprabha Coop. Sugar Factory Ltd. and Ors. vs. Union of India (UOI) and Ors. (16.11.2000 - SC) : MANU/ SC/2520/2000

Relative Section:

Essential Commodities Act, 1955 - Section 3(3c)

Hon'bleJudges/Coram:

B.N. Kirpal, N. Santosh Hegde and Doraiswamy Raju

Equivalent Citation: 2001 (43) ALR 72, 2001(2)BLJ335, JT2001(3)SC29, (2002)9SCC716

NumberofPagesintheOriginalJudgment: 2

Case Reference:

Shri Malaprabha Co-operative Sugar Factory Ltd. v. Union of India and Anr. MANU/SC/0306/1994

Case Note:

Civil - Fixation levy price - Section 3(3c) of Essential Commodities Act, 1955 - Petitioner filed that provisions of Clause 5A of Sugarcane Control Order had not taken into consideration while determined levy price - Hence, this Petition - Whether, Petitioners were entitled to increase in levy price up to full extent of amount paid under Clause 5A - Held, Clause 5A was incorporated in Sugarcane Control Order, which was instead of 100 percent of excess amount taken by Government, 50 per cent of excess went to cane grower and 50 percent was allowed to retained by sugar manufacturer - Thus, retention of 50 percent was a factor which could taken into consideration in determining Element (d) in Section 3(3C) of Act - However, that had been done, not to extent desired by Petitioners -Therefore, said fixation was in accordance with law and directions by Court had been complied - Therefore, it was neither a case for contempt nor any justification for given any direction to Government to refix levy price under Section 3(3C) of Act - - Petition Dismissed.

Ratio Decidendi: "Government shall take into consideration all aspect before fixation of levy price."

Facts:

1. In the present applications, it is contended that the petitioners were entitled to an increase in the levy price to the full extent of the amount paid under Clause 5A. For example, for West UP., the levy price fixed on 22nd February, 1995 was Rs. 163.780 and the revised levy price fixed by the Government, and impugned in these applications, is Rs. 172.430. According to the data furnished, the payment made under Clause 5A comes to Rs. 22.050. The contention of the petitioners is that this amount of Rs. 22.050 should have been added to the aforesaid amount of Rs. 163.780 and the final price which should have been fixed was Rs. 185.83.

Held by Hon'ble Court

We have heard the learned Counsel for the parties. The explanation given by the respondents is that prior to 1974 the entire excess realisation of the sale price of sugar at the end of the sugar year used to be taken by the Government. As a result of the Bhargava Committee's Report, Clause 5A was incorporated in the Sugarcane Control Order, the result of which was that instead of 100 per cent of the excess amount being taken by the Government 50 per cent of the excess went to the cane grower and 50 percent was allowed to be retained by the sugar manufacturer. In this way the sugar manufacturer benefited by retaining at least 50 per cent of the excess realisation whereas prior to 1974 the entire excess realisation used to go to the Government.

7. This Court in the aforesaid two decisions has said that the retention of 50 per cent is a factor which can be taken into consideration in determining the Element; (d) in Section 3(3C) of the Essential Commodities Act. The working statement given before us shows that this has been done, not to the extent as desired by the petitioners, but the result of this is that the levy price fixed at Rs. 163.780 in respect of west U.P. has gone up to Rs. 172.430.

In our opinion, the said fixation is in accordance with law and the directions given by this Court have been complied with. Neither a case for contempt has been made out nor is there any justification, in our opinion, for giving any direction to the Government to refix the levy price under Section 3(3C) of the Essential Commodities Act.

8. The contempt petitions are, accordingly, dismissed. No costs

The Chief of Marketing (Marketing Division), Coal India Ltd. and Ors. vs. Mewat Chemicals and Tiny S.S.I. Coal Pulverision Unit and Ors. (26.03.200

Relative Section:

ESSENTIAL COMMODITIES ACT, 1955 - SECTION 3

Hon'bleJudges/Coram:

S.N. Variava and H.K. Sema

Equivalent Citation: 2004(18)AIC348, (SCSuppl)2004(4)CHN124, 2004(1)CLJ(SC)309, JT2004(5) SC522 , 2004(3)RCR(Civil)26, 2004(4)SCALE71, (2004)4SCC146, [2004]3SCR597

NumberofPagesintheOriginalJudgment: 9

Case Reference:

Coal India Ltd. v. Continental Transport and Construction Corporation,MANU/SC/0513/1997

Case Note:

Civil - Essential Commodities Act, 1955 - Section 3; Colliery Control Order - Allocation of Coal - Competency of Coal controller - Applications made by respondents for allotment of coal and linkages - Grant of linkage /quota of coal by Coal Controller - Issue of order by Ministry of Coal that

Coal Controller was not authorized to grant any long term linkages and that allotment of coal by coal controller was subject to instructions of Central government - Writ petition by respondents - Allowed - Appeal - Dismissed by High Court holding that Coal Controller was competent to grant linkage and he being a competent authority, Central government could not sit in review over order passed by Coal Controller - Appeal to Supreme Court - Held that although certain functions had been specifically given to coal controller - However control of Central government was all pervasive and coal controller was not an authority equal to Central government - Since Clause 12A of colliery Control order clearly stipulated that coal controller was bound by instructions issued by Central government from time to time, and since coal controller being bound by circular dated 5th January, 1995 could not have given linkages - Where power to issue subsequent instructions having being categorically provided for in clause 12A, High Court erred in holding that order passed by Central government amounted to review - Order of coal controller and impugned judgments of courts below set aside

Industry: Chemicals

Facts: Briefly stated the facts are as follows:

1.In pursuance of the power under Section 3 of the Essential Commodities Act, 1955 the Colliery Control Order was framed. Under Clause 12A of the Colliery Control Order the Central Government could by Notification specify the authorities competent to allot quota of coal to any person or class of persons. Clause 12A further provides that every such authority shall allot coal subject to such instructions as the Central Government may issue from time to time.

2. On 25th June, 1992 the Central Government issued a Notification specifying the Coal Controller ac the competent authority to allot coal. On 5th January, 1995 a Circular was issued by the Central Government specifying that Coal India Ltd. would give coal clearances/linkages to the new applicants up to 5,000 tones per month and applications for more than 5,000 tones per month were to be decided by the Ministry of Coal. This Circular also specified that no allocation of coal could be made to private cookeries from any mines that are linked to washeries.

3. It appears that the Respondents had made applications for allotment of coal and had also applied for linkages. As their applications were not decided they filed Writ Petitions which were disposed off by an Order dated 25th September, 1995. The Coal Controller was directed to consider

the representations of the Respondents within 6 weeks. On 8th January, 1996 the Joint Secretary (Coal), New Delhi sent a fax message to the Coal Collector setting out that the Order of the High Court had not been complied with. It was pointed out that the Coal Controller was not vested with the power to give linkages, but that he could allot quota of coal. The Coal Controller was requested to intimate the latest position.

Held by Hon'ble Court

1. In our view, the High court was also in error in concluding that the position prevailing on the date of the application must apply. It is settled law that there is no vested right when a person makes an application. The position prevailing at the time the allotment is to apply. Before the allotment was made the Circular dated 5th January, 1995 had already been issued. The Coal Controller whilst allotting was bound to take note of that Circular. The Joint Secretary by his fax dated 8th January, 1996 had brought it to the notice of the Coal Controller. Thereafter guidelines had also been issued on 23rd April, 1996. The Coal Controller was bound to take note of those guidelines also. We are unable to understand the reasoning given by the High Court that those guidelines had been issued by a Director and thus could not be said to be guidelines Issued by the Central Government. These guidelines have been issued by the Ministry of Coal. Merely because they are forwarded not by a Joint Secretary but by a Director would not mean that they are not binding on the Coal Controller. If there was any doubt as to whether they had been issued by the Central Government, the Coal Controller should have asked for clarification from the Central Government.

2. In the above view, we find ourselves unable to sustain the Order of the single Judge or the Division Bench. They are accordingly set aside. The Writ Petitions filed by the Respondents stand dismissed.

3. It is submitted that the Appellants had deposited monies with ECL in June 1998. It is submitted that those monies are still lying with ECL. It is submitted that ECL should now deliver the coal. It was very fairly stated by Mr. Salve that ECL would deliver D grade coal subject to the requirements of power sector and subject to availability of D grade coal.

4. It was further submitted that monies have also been deposited with NCL and against those monies coal should be supplied. However, those monies were deposited pending this Appeal. They were deposited knowing fully well that if the Appeal is decided against the Respondents they would not be allotted coal from NCL. As the order of the Coal Controller has been

set aside the Respondents have no right to receive coal from NCL. therefore, they are not entitled to any coal from NCL. Thus NCL is directed to return the monies to the Respondents within 15 days from today.

5. The Appeal stands disposed of accordingly. There will be no order as to costs.

Adv. Jayprakash Somani's Videos On Law

Adv. Jayprakash Somani's Videos on Law on Youtube- 'jaysomani64' channel.

1) SLP in Supreme Court / Special Leave Petitions in the Supreme Court of India

2) Transfer of Civil & Criminal Cases by the Supreme Court of India / Transfer of Matrimonial Cases

3) Appellate Jurisdiction of the Supreme Court of India

4) Jurisdictions of the Supreme Court of India

5) Public Interest Litigation in the Supreme Court of India / PIL in Supreme Court

6) Article 32 Writ Petitions in the Supreme Court of India

7) Bail Matters Top 10 Supreme Court Cases

8) FIR Quashing in High Court & Supreme Court

9) Bail & Anticipatory Bail Matters in Supreme Court

10) Insolvency & Bankruptcy Matters in the Supreme Court

11) Insolvency & Bankruptcy Code 2016 Part 1

12) Insolvency & Bankruptcy Code 2016 Part 2

13) Insolvency & Bankruptcy Code 2016 Part 3

14) Corporate Liquidation Process

15) Supreme Court Rules & Procedures Webinar of 2.5 hour on Zoom

16) RDDBFI Act, 1993 (Introduction)

17) The Indian Contact Act 1872

18) Negotiable Instruments Act (Introduction)

19) How to avoid matrimonial disputes& some more videos

20) SEBI Matters in the Supreme Court

21) Matrimonial Matters: Supreme Court's 20 Case Laws

22) Consumer Matters Supreme Court's 20 Case Laws

23) Service Matters Supreme Court's 20 Case Laws

24) How to Search Lawyer for Your Matter

25) Property Matters Supreme Court's 20 Case Laws

26) Bail Matters: Supreme Court's 20 Case Laws

27) Supreme Court / High Court Vacation Benches

28) 69000 Teacher's Recruitment Matters of UP Government in the Supreme Court

29) Contempt of Court Matters in the Supreme Court

30) Advocate Act's Matters in the Supreme Court

31) Business Law Matters in the Supreme Court

32) Banking Matters in the Supreme Court

33) Labour Law Matters in the Supreme Court

34) Arbitration Matters in the Supreme Court

35) Careers in Law -Zoom Webinar by Adv. Jayprakash Somani

36) Civil Matters in the Supreme Court

37) Consumer Protection Act | Consumer Matters in the Supreme Court

38) Corporate Matters in the Supreme Court

39) Criminal Matters in the Supreme Court

40) Role of Respondent in the Supreme Court of India

41) Motor Vehicle Accident Matters in Supreme Court with case laws

42) Article 131 Original Suits in Supreme Court

43) PIL in Supreme Court/ Public Interest Litigations in the Supreme Court of India'

44) CAB Citizenship Amendment Bill is not Unconstitutional

45) Supreme Court of India Cases & Process – Marathi

46) Legal Services Export / Export of Legal Services

47) Transfer of Matrimonial Cases by the Supreme Court of India

48) Public Interest Litigation PIL

49) The Specific Relief Act (Introduction)

50) Corporate Insolvency Resolution Process CIRP

51) ABMM's Career 5 - Careers in Law

52) Transfer of cases by Supreme Court

53) Writ Petitions in High Court & Supreme Court of India

54) Supreme Court Jurisdictions - Appeals, SLP, Writ Petitions, Transfer, Original, Review, Curative

55) LEGAL INDIA TV Show: Cases Handled in Supreme Court

56) Corporate Liquidation Process

57) Legal Services Export / Export of Legal Services

58) Corporate Laws

59) Election Matters- Supreme Court's 20 Case Laws

60) Companies Act, 2013

62) Competition Act, 2002

63) Banking Matters - Supreme Court's 20 Case Laws

64) Election Matters in the Supreme Court

65) Armed Forces Tribunal Matters in the Supreme Court

66) Compassionate Appointment Service matter

67) Foreign Exchange Management Act FEMA

68) Foreign Trade Policy 2021-26 Proposed

69) Customs Act 1962

70) Narcotic Drugs and Psychotropic Substances Act, 1985 NDPS Act

71) Foreign Trade Development & Regulation Act, 1992

72) How to Search Good Advocate in the Supreme Court of India

73) Sr. Adv Vikas Singh's Interview in Nani Palkhivala Wednesday Law Club

74) Indian Penal Code (I. P. C.)

75) Criminal Procedure Code (Cr. P. C.)

76) Commercial Courts & International Arbitration - by Mr. Jaideep Gupta, Senior Advocate in Nani Palkhivala Wednesday Law Club

77) Sr. Adv Ranji Thomos in Nani Palkhivala Wednesday Law Club

78) Urgent Matters in Supreme Court during vacations

79) 498A Bail Matters in Supreme Court

81) 376 Bail Matters in Supreme Court

82) 302, 304, 307, 308 Bail Matters in Supreme Court

83) 138, 420 Bail Matters in Supreme Court

84) POCSO Act Bail Matters in Supreme Court

85) NDPS Act Bail Matters in Supreme Court

86) What is ED (Enforcement Directorate)?

87) Prevention of Money Laundering Act, 2002 (PMLA Act)

88) Insolvency & Bankruptcy Code- Supreme Court Case Laws. Webinar in Nani Palkhivala Wednesday Law Club

89) What is NCLT & NCLAT?

90) Acquittal from 376- Supreme Court's some case laws in Nani Palkhivala Wednesday Law Club dt 28.7.22

91) Insolvency & Bankruptcy in India

92) Can we file case directly in the Supreme Court?

93) Adv. Anuja Pethia has cleared AOR Exam 2021 with 77% marks - Her interview in Nani Palkhivala Wednesday Law Club

94) Customs Act - Supreme Court Case Laws & Interview of AOR Adv. Anuja Pethia in Nani Palkhivala Law Club.

95) The Uttar Pradesh Public Service Tribunals Act, 1976

96) POCSO Act - Supreme Court Case Laws & Interview of AOR Adv. Shoumendu Mukharji & Adv. Nishant Verma in Nani Palkhivala Law Club.

97) Who Can Trigger CIRP Process Under Insolvency Law of India

98) The Uttar Pradesh Government Servant Discipline and Appeal Rules, 1999

99) CIRP Application Under Sec 7 by FC

100) Information Technology Act 2000

101) Uttar Pradesh Recruitment of Dependants of Government Servants Dying in Harness Rules, 1974

102) Foreign Exchange Management Act 1999 & Supreme Court's Case Laws on FEMA & Leading Case of AOR Exam in Nani Palkhivala Law Club.

103) Arbitration and Conciliation Act 1996 & It's Supreme Court Case Laws in Nani Palkhivala Wednesday Law Club.

104) Narcotic Drugs & Psychotropic Substances Act 1985 (NDPS Act) & It's Supreme Court Case Laws in Nani Palkhivala Wednesday Law Club.

105) Recovery of Debts and Bankruptcy Act 1993

106) Uttar Pradesh Land Revenue Code 2006

107) CIRP Application Under Sec 9 by OC

108) CIRP Application Under Sec 10 by CD

109) Hindu Succession Act, 1956

110) Maharashtra Civil Services Rules, 1981

111) Indian Contract Act, 1872 & Supreme Court's Case Laws" in Nani Palkhiwala Wednesday Law Club

112) Securities and Exchange Board of India Act, 1992 i. e. SEBI Act 1992 & Case Laws on Insiders Trading" in Nani Palkhiwala Wednesday Law Club

113) Moratorium Under Section 14 of IBC, 2016

114) Hindu Marriage Act, 1955

115) Maharashtra Land Revenue Code, 1966

116) 64 Leading Cases of AOR Exam Session 1 :- Cases 1 to16 in Nani Palkhiwala Wednesday Law Club

117) 64 Leading Cases of AOR Exam Session 2: Cases 17 to 32 in Nani Palkhiwala Wednesday Law Club

118) 64 Leading Cases of AOR Examination Session 3: Cases 33 to 48 in Nani Palkhiwala Wednesday Law Club

119) 64 Leading Cases of AOR Exam Session 4: Cases 49 to 64 in Nani Palkhiwala Wednesday Law Club

120) Labour Laws of India: Part 1 - 4 New Labour Law Codes of India

121) New Labour Laws Part 2 The Code on Wages, 2019

122) New Labour Laws Part 3:- The Code on Social Security, 2020

123) Argue in English Fluently & Confidently - Two months online course.

124) SLP Admission in the Supreme Court. 2023 (Hindi)

125) Transfer of Petitions from the Supreme Court (Hindi)

126) Review Petition in the Supreme Court.(Hindi)

127) Recovery of debts from the Company (Hindi)

128) How to search 'Good Insolvency & Bankruptcy Consultant?' (HINDI)

129) Curative Petition in the Supreme Court

130) AFT Appeals in the Supreme Court (HINDI)

131) NCLAT's Appeals in the Supreme Court.

132) Transfer Petition: Which matters can we transfer?

133) SLP Types of SLP in the Supreme court of India (English).

134) Argue in English Fluently and Confidently in the High Court & Supreme Court'.

List Of Adv. Jayprakash Somani's Published Books

1. Supreme Court of India's Leading Case Laws on 'Insolvency & Bankruptcy Code 2016'

2. Bail Matters – Supreme Court's Latest Leading Case Laws

3. Arbitration Matters- Supreme Court's Latest Leading Case Laws

4. Property Matters - Supreme Court's Latest Leading Case Laws

5. Matrimonial Matters- Supreme Court's Latest Leading Case Laws

6. Election Matters- Supreme Court's Latest Leading Case Laws

7. SEBI Matters- Supreme Court's Latest Leading Case Laws

8. Banking Matters- Supreme Court's Latest Leading Case Laws

9. Service Matters- Supreme Court's Latest Leading Case Laws

10. Contempt of Court Matters- Supreme Court's Latest Leading Case Laws

11. Consumer Protection Matters- Supreme Court's Latest Leading Case Laws

12. Corporate Law- Supreme Court's Latest Leading Case Laws

13. Supreme Court's AOR Exam- Leading Cases

14. Armed Force Tribunal - Supreme Court's Latest Leading Case Laws

15. Acquittal From 376 - Supreme Court's Latest Leading Case Laws

16. Negotiable instrument – Supreme Court's Latest Leading Case Laws

17. Contract Act- Supreme Court's Latest Leading Case Laws

18. Insider trading- Supreme Court's Latest Leading Case Laws

19. Foreign Exchange and Management Act- Supreme Court's Latest Leading Case Laws

20. Income Tax Act- Supreme Court's Latest Leading Case Laws

21. Company Law- Supreme Court's Latest Leading Case Laws

22. Competition & Monopoly Matters- Supreme Court's Latest Leading Case Laws

23. Compassionate Appointment- Service Matters- Supreme Court's Latest Leading Case Laws

24. Compulsory Retirement- Service Matters- Supreme Court's Latest Leading Case Laws

25. Voluntary Retirement- Service Matters- Supreme Court's Latest Leading Case Laws

26. Removal/Dismissal/Termination from Service- Supreme Court's Latest Leading Case Laws

27. Seniority- Service Matter- Supreme Court's Latest Leading Case Laws

28. Promotion- Service Matter- Supreme Court's Latest Leading Case Laws

29. Equal Pay for Equal Work- Service Matter- Supreme Court's Latest Leading Case Laws

30. Condition of Service- Service Matter- Supreme Court's Latest Leading Case Laws

31. Customs Act- Supreme Court's Leading Case Laws

32. Information Technology Act- Supreme Court's Leading Case Laws

33. SEC. 125 CR. P. C.- Supreme Court's Leading Case Laws

34. SEC. 498A OF I. P. C.- Supreme Court's Leading Case Laws

35. MOTOR VEHICLE ACT- Supreme Court's Leading Case Laws

36. CONDITION OF SERVICE- SERVICE MATTER- Supreme Court's Leading Case Laws

37. SUSPENSION- SERVICE MATTER- Supreme Court's Leading Case Laws

38. Reservation in SC, ST, OBC- Service Matter- Supreme Court's Leading Case Laws

39. NARCOTIC DRUGS AND PSYCHOTROPIC SUBSTANCES (NDPS) ACT - Supreme Court of India's Latest Leading Case Laws

40. SEC 302 IPC - Supreme Court of India's Latest Leading Case Laws

41. PROTECTION OF CHILDREN FROM SEXUAL OFFENCES ACT (POCSO) - Supreme Court of India's Latest Leading Case Laws

42. PMLA ACT BAIL MATTERS - Supreme Court of India's Leading Case Laws

43. SEC 376 BAIL MATTERS - Supreme Court of India's Leading Case Laws

44. SEC 302 BAIL MATTERS - Supreme Court of India's Leading Case Laws

45. POCSO ACT BAIL MATTERS - Supreme Court of India's Leading Case Laws

46. JUVENILE JUSTICE ACT- Supreme Court of India's Leading Case Laws

47. TRANSFER OF PROPERTY ACT- Supreme Court of India's Leading Case Laws

48. PROFESSIONAL ETHICS OF ADVOCATES- AOR EXAM- SUPREME COURT'S LEADING CASE LAWS

49. WHITE COLLAR CRIME- SUPREME COURT'S LEADING CASE LAWS

50. SEC 302 BAIL MATTERS- SUPREME COURT'S LEADING CASE LAWS

51. SEC 7 IBC 2016 - SUPREME COURT'S LATEST LEADING CASE LAW

52. ADVERSE POSSESSION IN PROPERTY MATTER - SUPREME COURT'S LATEST LEADING CASE LAWS

53. ARMED FORCE TRIBUNAL ACT- SUPREME COURT'S LATEST LEADING CASE LAWs

Books are available online in India

1. Notion Press: https://notionpress.com/author/jayprakash_somani

2. Amazon: https://www.amazon.in/s?k=jayprakash+somani

3. Flipkart: https://www.flipkart.com/search?q=Jayprakash%20Somani

Books are available online at International Market

4. Amazon International: https://www.amazon.com/s?k=jayprakash+somani

5. Amazon United Kingdom: https://www.amazon.co.uk/s?k=jayprakash+somani

6. E-Books/Kindle edition at National & International Level: https://www.amazon.in/s?k=jaypraksh+somani

Adv Jayprakash Somani's Online Courses

Download our app to get access to our Free Videos, Free Bare Acts, Free Study Material in Legal as well as International Business Regime.

Android App Link ;-https://clpandrea.page.link/cmSm

Ios APp Link :-https://apps.apple.com/us/app/classplus/id1324522260

Login with org code ;- (qywzji)

Web Link ;-https://qywzji.courses.store/

Download App on Google play store - Type

<u>Jayprakash Somani SupremeCourt</u>

Legal Courses :

1. **SLP- Bail Matters- Drafting & Successful Arguing in the Supreme Court.**

Description -This Course is helpful to Advocates, Litigants, Law Officers, Law Students, Law Schools, Individual. Course contains 8 Videos + Study Material+ PDF Books. Access to this course is for Two Years. Expected duration of this course is one month only.

Topics : 1. SLP- Bail Matters- Drafting & Successful Arguing in the Supreme Court, **2.** Types of bails, **3.** Laws related to bail matters, **4.** How to read Impugned Order of High Court & frame substantial question of laws, **5.** How to draft excellent SLP,**6.** Searching of citations/ case laws, **7.** How to argue in admission hearings, **8.** How argue in after notice hearing.

Speaker: Jayprakash Bansilal Somani, MBA (Foreign Trade), LL. B. Advocate, Supreme Court of India & IP www.jayprakashsomani.com Call: P. A. 9322188701

2. SLP- Succession Matters- Drafting & Successful Arguing in the Supreme Court.

Description - This Course is helpful to Advocates, Litigants, Law Officers, Law Students, Law Schools, Individual. Course contains 9 Videos + Study Material+ PDF Books. Access to this course is for Two Years. Expected duration of this course is one month only.

Topics :1. SLP- Succession Matters- Drafting & Successful Arguing in the Supreme Court,**2.** Information about Succession Matters,**3.** Laws related to Succession Matters, **4.** How to read Impugned Order of High Court to frame substantial questions of law, **5.** How to draft excellent synopsis & list of date, **6.** Drafting of SLP of Succession Matter, **7.** Searching of citations/ case laws, **8.** How to prepare notes & then argue in admission hearings, **9.** How to prepare notes & then argue in after notice final hearing.

Speaker: Jayprakash Bansilal Somani, MBA (Foreign Trade), LL. B. Advocate, Supreme Court of India & IP www.jayprakashsomani.com Call: P. A. 9322188701

3. Legal Vocabulary & its practice pattern to Argue in High Court and Supreme Court / Improve Your Legal English

Description - This Course is helpful to Advocates, Litigants, Law Officers, Law Students, Law Schools, Individual. Course contains 11 Videos + Study Material+ PDF Books. Access to this course is for Two Years. Expected duration of this course is three month only.

Topics : **1.** Legal Vocabulary & its practice pattern to Argue in High Court and Supreme Court / Improve Your Legal English, **2.** 1000 legal verbs with its three forms, **3.** Twelve Tenses with its running practice, **4.** One Pdf book on legal vocabulary & its practice pattern with Latin Terms, **5.** Second Pdf book on legal vocabulary & its practice pattern with Latin Terms, **6.** Some Videos of CJI Dr. Dhananjay Chandrachud for the practice of good legal English, **7.** Some Video/Audio Lectures of Legend Nani Palkhivala for standard perfect legal English & flow of Speech, **8.** Some Videos of renowned Sr. Advocates from Mumbai for flow, legal vocabulary & their struggle in legal journey, **9.** Some Videos of Sr. Advocates of the Supreme Court for flow & legal vocabulary,**10.** Some Videos of foreign persons to improve Professional English & thinking process in English,**11.** Some important legal doctrines with case laws.

Speaker: Jayprakash Bansilal Somani, MBA (Foreign Trade), LL. B. Advocate, Supreme Court of India & IP www.jayprakashsomani.com Call: P. A. 9322188701.

4. SLP- Property Matters - Drafting and Successful Arguing in the Supreme Court.

Description - This Course is helpful to Advocates, Litigants, Law Officers, Law Students, Law Schools 8 Individual. Course contains 9 Videos + Study Material+ PDF Books. Access to this course is for Two Years. Expected duration of this course is one month only.

Topics : 1. SLP- Property Matters - Drafting and Successful Arguing in the Supreme Court, **2.** Types of Property Matters, **3.** Laws related to Property Matters, **4.** How to read Impugned Order of High Court to guide client & frame substantial question of laws, **5.** How to draft Synopsis & List of Dates in Property Matter, **6.** How to draft excellent SLP of Property Matter, **7.** Searching of citations/ case laws with specific paras, **8.** How to argue confidently in admission hearings, **9.** How argue confidently in after notice & final hearings.

Speaker: Jayprakash Bansilal Somani, MBA (Foreign Trade), LL. B. Advocate, Supreme Court of India & IP www.jayprakashsomani.com Call: P. A. 9322188701.

International Business Courses -

1. Agri Products Exports - Scope from India.

Description - This Course is helpful to Agriculturalists, Entrepreneurs, Exporters, Importers, Students. Course contains 12 Videos + Study Material+ PDF Books. Access to this course is for Two Years. Expected duration of this course is one month only.

Topics : **1-** Agri Products Exports - Scope from India,**2.** Agri Export's share in India's total export, **3.** Agri Export Promotional Council's Support, **4.** Top 10 Agri export countries, **5.** Top 10 Agri export product, **6.** India's share in World's Agri Exports, **7.** Onion Exports from India, **8.** Rice Exports from India, **9.** Mango Exports from India, **10.** Fresh Vegetable Exports, **11.** Fresh Fruits Exports, **12.** Export of Agri Allied Products.

Speaker: Jayprakash Bansilal Somani, MBA (Foreign Trade), LL. B. Advocate, Supreme Court of India & IP www.jayprakashsomani.com Call: P. A. 9322188701.

2. Textile Exports - Scope from India.

Description -This Course is helpful to Textile Business Houses, Entrepreneurs, Exporters, Importers, Students. Course contains 14 Videos

+ Study Material+ PDF Books. Access to this course is for Two Years. Expected duration of this course is one month only.

Topics :1- Textile Exports - Scope from India, 2. Textile Export's share in India's total exports, 3. Support of Textile Export Promotional Council, 4. Top 10 Countries in Textile Exports, 5. Top 10 Products in Textile Exports, 6. Export of Readymade Garments, 7. Export of Man-made Textiles, 8. Export of Handloom Products, 9. Export of Wool & Woollen Textiles, 10. Export of Silk, 11. Exports of Handicrafts & Carpets, 12. Exports of Coir & Coir Manufacturers, 13. Exports of Jute,14. India's share in World's total textile expor.

Speaker: Jayprakash Bansilal Somani, MBA (Foreign Trade), LL. B. Advocate, Supreme Court of India & IP www.jayprakashsomani.com Call: P. A. 9322188701.

3. Export Import Procedure -Perfect Documentation & It's Management.

Description -This Course is helpful to Business Men, Service Providers, Entrepreneurs, Exporters, Importers, Students. Course contains 13 Videos + Study Material+ PDF Books. Access to this course is for Two Years. Expected duration of this course is three months only.

Topics : 1. Export Import Procedure, Perfect Documentation & Its management, 2. Company Formation, 3. Opening of Bank Account in AD Bank, 4. Export Procedure points, 5. Import Procedure Points, 6. Taking Import Export Code, 7. Taking RCMC number,8. Registration at Port when necessary, 9. Quality Inspection Certificate of Goods, 10. CHA & its roll, 11. Custom Formalities, 12. Export Documents such as Invoice, Bill of Lading, Insurance Certificate, Quality Inspection Certificate & others, 13. Excellent Management of Export & Imports Documents.

Speaker: Jayprakash Bansilal Somani, MBA (Foreign Trade), LL. B. Advocate, Supreme Court of India & IP www.jayprakashsomani.com Call: P. A. 9322188701.

4. Jewellery Exports -Scope from India

Description - You can understand world wide scope for Jems & Jewellery in multidimensional ways. 14 videos of this course will create positive spark among you to enter into the Exports & Imports of Gems & Jewellery and other products. Chance to ask your query to Somani Sir every week.

Topics :1. Jewellcry Exports - Scope from India, 2. Jewellery Export's share in India's total exports, 3. Support of Jems & Jewellery Export

Promotional Council, **4.** Top 10 Countries in Jewellery Exports, **5.** Top 10 Products in Jewellery Exports, **6.** Export of Cut & Polished Diamonds, **7.** Export of Gold Jewellery, **8.** Export of Plain Gold Jewellery, **9.** Export of Studded Gold Jewellery, **10.** Export of Silver Jewellery, **11.** Exports of Platinum Jewellery, **12.** Exports of Imitation Jewellery, **13.** Exports of Articles of Gold, Silver & others,**14.** India's share in World's total Jewellery export.

Speaker: Jayprakash Bansilal Somani, MBA (Foreign Trade), LL. B. Advocate, Supreme Court of India & IP www.jayprakashsomani.com Call: P. A. 9322188701.

5. Export Import Finance Management with LC, ECGC & Venture Capital.

Description -You can understand A to Z about International Finance with LC, ECGC & Venture Capital in simple language & with illustrations. 11 videos of this course will create positive spark among you regarding International Finance Management with practical tips. Chance to ask your query to Somani Sir every week.

Topics : 1. Export Import Finance Management with LC, ECGC & Venture Capital, **2.** Which is good & excellent source of finance, **3.** Banking Finance, **4.** List of Banks which provides finance for International Business, **5.** How to start business in Less or Zero Capital, **6.** Letter of Credit, **7.** Types of LCs **8.** Scrutiny of L/C, **9.** ECGC Policy, **10.** Venture Capital Finance., **11.** Ideal formula of Investment & continues growth.

Speaker: Jayprakash Bansilal Somani, MBA (Foreign Trade), LL. B. Advocate, Supreme Court of India & IP www.jayprakashsomani.com Call: P. A. 9322188701.

6. Shipping & Logistics in International Business with live links of Ports, ICDs, CHAs etc.

Description -This Course is helpful to any Businessman, Professionals, Entrepreneurs, Exporters, Importers, CHAs, & Students.

Course contains following 10 Videos + Study Material+ PDF Books. Access to this course is for Two Years. Expected duration of this course is three months only.

Topics : 1. Shipping & Logistics in International Business with live links of Ports, ICDs, CHAs etc, **2.** Roll of CHA in Shipping & Logistics of International Business, **3.** How to find good & genuine CHA, **4.** Courier/ post service for small parcel, **5.** India's important Ports & ICDs with live links, **6.** How & what to study Ports/ ICDs websites, **7.** Art to reduce charges of Shipping & logistics, **8.** Information about some Top International Ports with live links, **9.** Roll of Customs in Exports & Imports,**10.** How to become CHA .

Speaker: Jayprakash Bansilal Somani, MBA (Foreign Trade), LL. B. Advocate, Supreme Court of India & IP www.jayprakashsomani.com Call: P. A. 9322188701.

7. International Business Marketing Part 1: Finding Potential & Genuine Buyers for Exports and Suppliers for Imports.

Description -You can understand Seven Excellent ways to Find Potential & Genuine Buyers for Exports and Suppliers for Imports with illustrations. 11 videos of this course will create positive spark among you regarding International Business Marketing with practical tips. Chance to ask your query to Somani Sir every week.

Topics : 1. International Business Marketing Part 1: Finding Potential & Genuine Buyers for Exports and Suppliers for Imports,**2.** Seven Excellent Ways to find Potential Buyers for Exports, **3.** Top 20 B to B Websites in the World, **4.** Searching Potential Buyers from B to B Sites. Is this safe & good way to search potential buyers, **5.** Searching Potential Buyers through Export Promotional Councils & Its Magazines, **6.** Searching Potential Buyers with help from Embassies, **7.** Searching Potential Buyers through Chamber of Commerce at global level, **8.** Searching Potential Buyers from International Trade Fairs & Exhibitions, **9.** Searching Potential Buyers through your friends & relatives or any Indian Person in focus countries, **10.** How to find focus countries for your products or services, **11.** Taking references from establish buyer/seller.

Speaker: Jayprakash Bansilal Somani, MBA (Foreign Trade), LL. B. Advocate, Supreme Court of India & IP www.jayprakashsomani.com Call: P. A. 9322188701.

8. International Business Marketing Part 2: Communication Skill to take repeated orders from Potential Buyers

Description - You can learn Perfect Communication Skills to initiate International Trade with foreign buyers and art to take repeated orders from these Potential Buyers with illustrations. 11 videos of this course will create positive spark among you to reach upto One Star Exporter Level rapidly and subsequent journey to reach upto Five Star Export House. Chance to ask your query to Somani Sir every week.

Topics :1. International Business Marketing Part 2: Communication Skill to take repeated orders from Potential Buyers,**2.** Preparation of

Impressive Company Profile, **3.** Excellent Product CatLog for International Market, **4.** Phone Calls with maintaining dignity of ourself & our country, **5.** Sending emails, **6.** Sending what's app messages, **7.** Technique of repeated follow up, **8.** Art of taking 100% advance payments, **9.** Before giving credit facility how to look credibility of potential buyers or suppliers, **10.** Art of earning good profit of margin, **11.** Art of managing international clients.

Speaker: Jayprakash Bansilal Somani, MBA (Foreign Trade), LL. B. Advocate, Supreme Court of India & IP www.jayprakashsomani.com Call: P. A. 9322188701.